GOD HAS GIVEN US EVERY GOOD THING

GOD
HAS GIVEN US
EVERY GOOD
THING

ROY EUGENE DAVIS

CSA PRESS, *Publishers*
Lakemont, Georgia 30552

Dedicated to

PARAMAHANSA YOGANANDA

who accepted me as I was, and
whose life transmitted to me
the reality of the true Self.

and to

EVERY PERSON

whose life has touched mine.
God, through you, has made
a difference.

FOREWORD

We have come into this world from deep inner space, and to deep inner space we will eventually return. We have come into the world in order to participate in the drama of life and to be representatives of the Divine Will in the process.

The major opportunity available to every human being is that of awakening from the hypnotic-like trance of unknowingness, in order to directly perceive and comprehend ultimate reality. Until the moment of grace, if we are reasonably conscious, we have a choice in the matter: we can choose to do what we can to prepare for our spiritual awakening, or we can choose to continue in a routine of mundane concerns, involvements and relationships. Once we are touched by grace, however, we have no choice but to surrender to God's will for us, which is soul awakening and illumination of consciousness.

God does not cause human suffering, nor does God cause human happiness. Suffering, or the absence of it, is the result of man's own mental states and states of consciousness. Therefore, each person, if he is intent upon the spiritual quest, can learn to perceive without errors and live without restrictions.

We err if we are lulled into believing that personal fulfillment is determined by externals, by harmonious relationships, personal achievement, or the accumulation of material things and a multitude of sensory experiences. The truth is that if we are inwardly centered, inwardly illumined, all that is required for our experience of fulfilled living in this world is readily available to us. Indeed, when we are possessed of understanding, we can testify that *God has given us every good thing.*

In that marvelous portion of the Gospel According to Saint Matthew designated as The Sermon on the Mount, Jesus taught (Matthew 6:33), "But seek ye first the kingdom of God and His righteousness, and all these things shall be added unto you." This is the central message: seek the Giver, not the gifts; seek the Source, not the outer effects; seek the knowledge of God and everything else will be revealed.

It is normal for one to desire to be happy, to be healthy, to be prosperous, to be God-conscious. When conditions are ideal with us we will glorify God in the world. The key to this end is to be inwardly anchored in the realization of God, while living a useful life in relationship to others and the world process.

To be a human being is to be a blend of divine qualities and mind and body. Mental and physical characteristics are subject to change because they are part of relative manifestation. The inner essence, the soul, which is a specialized expression of the Larger Life, is birthless, deathless, and immortal. When we live out of soul awareness we live in this world, but we are not overly influenced by it.

I cannot recall a time when I was not inwardly aware of being a ray of God. I have always, from childhood, sensed and felt the presence of a benevolent *something* within and around me, a reality which is supportive, nourishing, and caring. In conversations with people, over the years and in many parts of the world, many have shared with me their own inner feelings about their divine nature, and about their awareness of a caring presence. Why is it that so many people sense the truth about themselves and about God? Can it be that man is able to intuitively know his real nature, and his relationship with God? Of course, this is so. I am convinced that every rational person wants to know the final truth about life, about God, the soul and the universe. We do not yearn for knowledge without purpose; we yearn to know the truth because of the innate inclination of the soul, which is extending itself to experience omnipresence and omnipotence. Without this knowing, without this conscious realization, we can never feel whole and complete. It was this yearning to know the truth about life which caused me to inquire into the nature of consciousness at an early age, and which led me to my guru, Paramahansa Yogananda. Finally, it resulted in a ministry which has been able to touch the lives of multiplied thousands of men, women and children around the globe.

The dedicated scientist and the contemplative mystic are both engaged in an examination of the nature of reality. Eventually they must perceive the true nature of things and the order of the universe in the same way. There exist basic principles which undergird all natural phenomena. When these are known to him, all man's doubts are settled, all his questions answered, and all his problems forever solved.

Every great spiritual teacher has taught the inevitability of soul awakening and final freedom in God. Clear understanding of the nature of consciousness is helpful to one on the spiritual path; it is hoped that the reading of this material will be helpful to many sincere seekers. In the immortal classic, *The Bhagavad Gita*, Arjuna's final statement epitomizes the ideal understanding and attitude of a disciple:

> My delusion is banished now, and through the grace of God I recognize the Truth. I am stable now, with my doubts removed. I shall act according to these words of wisdom. (18:73)

Our initial quest for understanding may be prompted by a variety of motives. It may be that healing is needed, or an improvement in circumstances. It may be that fascination with esoteric matters proves the key factor. It may be that the urge to know God is predominant. Whatever the reason for our beginning on the path, sooner or later, if we are rightly resolved, the yearning for Self-realization will become the dominant urge.

Who can tell another person's destiny? We are born with urges, with tendencies and aptitudes which are unique to us alone, although similar to those of others. For some, the path will be arduous, requiring tremendous personal effort to prepare for the redeeming influx of divine power. For others, the way will be relatively easy, a matter of mere choice and accept-ance. For a few, those who are endowed with awakened in-tuition and keen powers of discernment, together with an almost total absence of ego-sense, life will be one spontaneous unfoldment after another and liberation of consciousness will be quickly experienced.

What determines this is fate and destiny. Fate is related to ingrained habits and tendencies, to desires and conditionings. Destiny, on the other hand, is a matter of grace, the activity of the Holy Spirit in, and through, one's life which moves irresistably in the direction of certain completion.

What a great blessing it is to be under grace! Grace is avail-able to all, but cannot be experienced unless there is a willing-ness to submit to a Power which is superior to our own when we are living from the human condition. We may understand and accept the teachings of the masters of the ages; we may believe fully and trust implicitly; yet, until we experience the very Life of God, we are empty. Fundamentalist Christians refer to the experience of God's Life as the infilling of the Holy Spirit. Yogis refer to it as the awakening of kundalini, the unrestricted movement of heretofore dormant soul poten-tial. However it is described, when the Life of God is apparent and influential, conditions are dramatically changed. What was before impossible is easily manifested. What before could not be done occurs without undue effort and in the most natural and orderly way.

"Hell" and "heaven" are reflections of states of conscious-ness. According to our state of consciousness we experience life. This is the simple truth of relative existence. Beyond states of consciousness is the experience of Being, during which no relative perception is present. But so long as we relate to the material worlds—to energy, primal particles, space, and time—we will have to live from states of consciousness.

It is essential that we be aware of the difference between the soul, the being, and the states of consciousness experienced by the soul. It is important that we know this for ourselves, and it is also helpful to us in our relationships with others. For ourselves, when we are not expressing the most ideal state of consciousness, we can inwardly be reassured by knowing that states of consciousness are transitory, while the real nature is always stable and pure. For others, when we observe sometimes erratic behavior in others, we can know that their behavior is a reflection of a temporary state of consciousness and that the real being is clear and perfect. In this manner we can live without harshly judging ourselves or others.

Is the guru-disciple relationship relevant today? Of course it is, for basic matters do not change with the times or with the shifting patterns of human thought. Should one depart from his present abode to seek a guru? No, all that is required is a closer walk with God and a prayer life surrendered to Him. Then, what happens will happen in the most ideal way. I have counseled hundreds of people (and I do not inflate the numbers) who have told me of their heartaches and misfortunes as a result of their having "gone on a pilgrimage to find their guru" only to return home, disenchanted and poorer in many ways. I have talked with dozens of people who thought they had found their connection, only to later find it shallow and nonuseful. Again, some have been used. A few were also able to admit that they recognized a useful contact but discovered themselves to be inadequate.

The true guru is Supreme Consciousness, That which is the cause and sustainer of the worlds, That which is the very Life of us all. The word *guru* means "teacher" as well as "light which removes darkness from the mind." God, as the true guru, moves into the human condition and dissolves it so that only His will is evident.

The true guru-disciple relationship will, I hope, be clearly evident as the following pages are read and understood. Let there be no mistake on this point: *the true guru is God.* An enlightened soul is but the personalized contact for God's influence. Any other seeming guru connection is false. And, unfortunately for some, and for the general public attitude, there have recently been published many accounts of incorrect and shameful pseudo-guru/disciple relationships. I will speak of this no further, because to do so would be but to fan the flames of ignorance.

The guru-disciple relationship has been a working tradition since the dance of life unfolded on the screen of time and space. We can always learn from those who know more than we. One of the more efficient routes to success in any endeavor is to live with, carefully observe, and experience with a master of whatever skill, trade or profession is involved. In this way do we learn, if we are teachable, everything the master knows. We can then move on from there.

I well remember the words of Paramahansaji, during a quiet interlude when he was encircled by disciples. It was early evening, and darkness had not yet fallen. He looked at us reflectively and said, "I do not want weak people around me. I want you to be as strong as I am!" We understood, then, that while we were to observe certain guidelines and be quick to obey requests, that he was teaching us how to be more God-like, more open to God's will.

The false notion of Eastern versus Western truth teaching must be transcended. Do we concern ourselves with the geographical location of scientific discovery? Of course not. The human condition and cultural differences are one thing; what is true about the nature of consciousness remains true regardless of the channel through whom truth is revealed. Pride and egocentricity must give way to understanding if we are to be citizens of the New Era.

One major contribution given to the world by yoga masters is that of calming the mind through the regulation of breathing patterns. There is an intimate relationship between breathing and mental activity. When breathing is diminished, vital forces in the body are regulated and thought processes become ordered. Eventually, during deep meditation, the contents of the mind become dormant and feelings become tranquil. The result is that, undisturbed by erratic emotional surges and mental activity, the meditator is able to experience unmodified, or pure, awareness.

The feeling nature of the mind causes it to seek experiences which result in pleasure or satisfaction of desires. When attention is constantly allowed to flow outward, the mind is forever involved with sensory experiences, sensations which cannot ever fully satisfy the soul. When attention is directed inward, however, during occasions of meditation and reflection, one is able to experience *beingness*, full soul satisfaction, which is far more satisfying than anything outer stimulation can provide.

When the mind is given the opportunity to experience pure consciousness, it naturally yearns to experience it more and more, and meditation becomes increasingly attractive to it. Repeated superconscious experience results in mental cleansing, emotional harmony, and improved body function. It is also possible, using meditation as a basis, to learn to regulate body processes which are usually considered to be involuntary, beyond one's ability to influence. Through the practice of certain meditation techniques, it is possible to refine the nervous system, awaken intuitive abilities, clear the faculty of intelligence, and regenerate the physical body. Such techniques have been practiced and taught for thousands of years by yoga masters and contemplatives of various esoteric traditions.

Intentional self-discipline, study of the nature of consciousness, and surrendering ego-sense in order to experience the Larger True Nature is the way to self-actualization and freedom. This has been known and taught for millenia; it is time-tested because of the experiences of hundreds of thousands of illumined seers. One's outer form of worship is personal and should be respected as such; the inner way is the same for all. It is the way of awakening and transcendence. The average person is at the mercy of the drives and tendencies which have roots in the deep unconscious. The awakened person's life is determined by superior influences which are grounded in the field of pure consciousness.

Physical birth and death are but minor incidents for the soul when a more cosmic view is experienced. Little does the average person know of his past experiences in this and other realms, and little does he suspect his true origin and certain destiny. Sooner or later all souls will awaken and consciously experience omnipresence. This cannot be avoided by any of us. We have come from the ocean of life and we will awaken to it at the right moment.

Planetary consciousness is being cleansed at a rapid rate,

and increasing numbers of men and women are coming to terms with their own spirituality and their relationship with God, the world, and each other. There is increasing evidence that more people are willing to assume responsibility for their lives and for the nourishment of the planet, and this is an indication of growing maturity.

I have written this book as a spiritual autobiography, to share with the reader some personal experiences and observations which may be helpful. Many years from now, as we review the course of our lives, let us be able to say, "I did my best to be open to God's goodness, and to help make this world a more congenial place for my brothers and sisters, and for future generations."

January 3, 1986
Lakemont, Georgia

CONTENTS

ILLUSTRATIONS

I salute the supreme teacher, the Truth,
whose nature is bliss, who is the giver
of the highest happiness, who is pure
wisdom, who is beyond all qualities and
infinite like the sky, who is beyond words,
who is one and eternal, pure and still,
who is beyond all change and phenomena
and who is the silent witness to all our
thoughts and emotions—I salute Truth,
the supreme teacher.

—Ancient Vedic Hymn

ONE

Early Years, and
Intimations of the Future

I was born about midnight, between March 8th and 9th, 1931. I was the fourth child of five, and the second son born to my parents. The place of my entry into the earth sphere was Leavittsburg, Ohio, and it was in this rural area of the northeastern region of the State that I grew up.

My father, DeWitt Talmage Davis, was named after a then-famous evangelist, because his mother had wanted him to be a minister. Father worked in a steel mill for some years, then bought a small farm, and also established a modest trucking business, hauling coal from the mines of Pennsylvania. He was a firm but fair parent, and set for his children a positive example of fair dealing, honest work, and faith in life.

My mother, Eva Lee Carter Davis, as did other farm women of that era, worked hard, performing all of the duties and chores necessary to see to the comfort and welfare of her family. When the family was together, and all chores had been attended to, she would play the piano and encourage us in joining her in the singing of familiar hymns and popular songs of the nineteen-forties.

From the time we moved to the farm when I was about six years of age, I was assigned chores which were to be completed correctly and punctually. I would help my older brother to clean the barns, feed the livestock, milk the cows and, in season, I helped with the planting and harvesting of field crops:

corn, wheat, oats, rye, and soybeans. There were also the annual projects of bringing the hay to the barns, cutting wood for the stove, and maintaining the fences surrounding the woods and pasture where the cows and horses roamed. We averaged about a dozen cows, and kept a team of workhorses.

Life on the farm was not all hard work. There was also ample time for fun and play: swimming in the creek in the summer, horseback riding, fishing, and hiking in the woods. I particularly enjoyed riding Flash, my bay stallion. I used a western stock saddle and, of course, wore cowboy boots and a western hat, purchased by mail from a firm in Dallas, Texas. My father, who learned the skill from his father, taught me to make a bow, and the arrows for it—how to carefully select the right wood, and season and shape it correctly. I also became a crack shot with an ancient Winchester rifle, which I used mainly for target shooting, because I was not overly attracted to the hunting of animals.

During the first two or three years on the farm, we did not have electricity. The house was heated in winter by a coal furnace and all the cooking was done on a large cast-iron wood stove in the kitchen. Water was drawn by hand from a well in the yard, using a bucket and rope, and carried to the house. Kerosene lamps were used for illumination in the house at night and lanterns were used during late evening farm chores. When electric lines were finally brought in, as part of the rural electrification program of the Federal government, what a difference it made in our lives! Now we had bright lights to read and work by, a refrigerator to keep food cool, and a radio to entertain the family and bring in news of the outside world, later including news of the impending Second World War which was to bring tragedy to so many millions of people before it would finally end in 1945.

Regular church attendance was the rule for every member of the family. We attended the United Brethren church about one mile from the farm. It had a total congregation of under one hundred adults and children. The church, a simple white wooden structure, was located near a sand quarry. This quarry was a source of concern to the local farmers; frequent dynamite blasts at the quarry altered the water table in the area, and wells and springs were affected. The processing of crushed sandstone also made the creek run yellow with mud for miles, until the fast-running water cleansed itself on its journey to the Mahoning River which ran through Leavittsburg.

Often, during the Sunday worship services, as the pastor preached his sermon, my attention wandered, and I turned to reflection upon man's relationship to God, my own relationship with God, and what the future held for me. In my mind's eye I saw myself as one of God's servants. When I heard stories of the Old Testament prophets, of Moses, Isaiah and Ezekiel, and of Jesus and the Apostles, my imagination soared. I wanted to be like them. With all my heart, I wanted God to use me for His purposes. These were interior visions and aspirations, and I shared them with no one else. My commitment to God was a very personal and private matter to me.

Shy and somewhat introverted, I seldom discussed philosophical ideas with my friends, but my personal prayer life became deeper and deeper, and I read selections from the Bible regularly. Whether working in the fields, walking in the woods, being involved with family activities, or alone in my room at night, I would be ever alert and watchful for signs of God's presence and leading. One night, when I was about fifteen, while attending a revival service at our church, I was led to respond to the altar call given by a visiting evangelist and, for the first time, I made a public commitment to the Christ of God. This was not a conversion experience, because I was already inwardly attuned to God, but it was an act of affirmation and a public declaration of my heretofore private commitment to God.

I attended school in Braceville, five miles from home. The average number of students in each class was two dozen, for each of the twelve grades. Grade school was interesting for me, and I had no problem with my studies. My special love was books, and I read voraciously and widely. During my high school years I had access to the school library, as well as the public library in Warren, the major city in Trumbull County, where I read every book available on psychology and Eastern

Philosophy. A daily newspaper, the *Warren Tribune*, was delivered to our home by mail, and it was in this newspaper that I first read of Father Divine, whom I was to meet many years later.

It was through the pages of a book I discovered in the school library that the world of yoga was opened to me. While reading *Lives of a Bengal Lancer* by Francis Yeats Brown, a personal account of the author's tour of duty as a soldier in India, I thrilled to his accounts of contacts with yogis. In the appendix the author included an outline of yogic systems and practices; this I avidly read and reread.

Continuing my search, I came across two more books which were helpful and fascinating. The first was Paul Brunton's *A Search in Secret India*, in which the author told of his visits to holy personages in that land often spoken of as "the mother of religions." One saint of whom he wrote was the great sage, Ramana Maharshi. *Maha* means "great" and *rishi* means "seer." As a young man, Ramana pondered the mystery of death. He experimented, lying down on the floor and imagining his own transition from the body. He discerned that even if the body were to cease functioning, and the mind no longer remain active, he would still be aware of awareness. Ramana left home, sought out a secluded place and underwent austere disciplines. Untrained in yogic processes, he prayed simply: "O Lord, consume me, as the spider consumes the fly!" He experienced spontaneous kundalini awakening, and was also directed from within to experience the most intricate yogic procedures. When his transformation was complete he retired to a cave on Arunachala Mountain, considered a sacred site, and there remained for the rest of his life. An ashram was built up around him by disciples, and people from all over the world sought him out, to imbibe his wisdom and experience his clear consciousness.

Another book which I read at about the same time was Theos Bernard's *Hatha Yoga*. This treatise provided me with specific information about the science of yoga, the guidelines for students on the path, and instructions for practicing asanas and pranayamas. Asanas, or yogic poses, are practiced in order to ensure bodily health, improved function of all systems, and to awaken dormant energies in preparation for deep meditation states to follow. Pranayama, sometimes referred to as the science of breath regulation, enables the practitioner to directly regulate vital forces in the body, and to quiet the mental processes.

At home, I experimented with yogic practices and soon discovered that I had a natural aptitude for them. Even the more intricate procedures were easily learned and mastered after a short period of practice. I would often sit in my bedroom on a blanket, assume a cross-legged posture, and pretend that I was a Himalayan yogi. Neither my family nor friends knew anything of my experiments with yogic procedures.

During the final years of high school I also became interested in body-building, training three times a week with a set of barbells which I purchased after saving enough money from my five-dollar monthly allowance. (My fantasy goal was to win the Mr. America contest in 1952!) I soon discovered that my body was not organized to produce massive musculature. In an attempt to gain body weight I consumed high protein meals, supplemented with large quantities of milk between meals.

In early 1949, during my senior year, I became ill. The diagnosis was rheumatic fever; I was confined to bed for the next five months. The family physician visited our home regularly to monitor my progress. No medication was prescribed, the only instruction being a regime of strict bed rest and a nourishing diet. I knew that my diet had been too rich in protein and felt that an internal cleansing was essential. Pouring through my collection of health magazines, I decided to change to a vegetarian diet, with emphasis upon fresh vegetables and fruit, especially those with a high vitamin C content.

This period of enforced seclusion proved, in the long run, to be very useful. It was during this time that I came across an advertisement in Bernarr MacFadden's *Physical Culture* magazine, in which Paramahansa Yogananda's amazing book, *Autobiography of a Yogi*, was offered. I had seen this advertisement a few months earlier but had not at that time followed through on my impulse to order it. This time, however, I did order the book, and in a week or two a copy was delivered by the mail carrier.

Autobiography of a Yogi became my second Bible. Paramahansaji's stories of saints, of miracles, of yogic procedures, held me enthralled as I read the book from cover to cover over and over again. As I looked at the photographs of Babaji, Lahiri Mahasaya, Swami Sri Yukteswar and Paramahansaji, I experienced a strong soul rapport. I *knew* them, and knew the spiritual states they had attained. I knew, too, that my life would continue to be blessed and enriched by the divine forces flowing through them to me, and to the world.

A short time later, I wrote a letter to the Self-Realization Fellowship, publishers of the book, and requested the weekly lessons which Paramahansaji had prepared for his students around the world. Soon I began to receive the lessons, and I diligently practiced the meditation procedures as described in them. Gradually I began to experience a deepening of my consciousness of God. At night, when the house was quiet, I prayed earnestly for inner guidance. I wanted to be well and strong, and to be able to travel to California to meet Paramahansaji.

At times, as I meditated, I would look into the spiritual eye and watch the ever-changing patterns of brilliant lights. One early evening as I prayed, lying on my back in bed, a force suddenly flooded my spine, causing the spinal column to arch and pulling my attention fully into the spiritual eye center. Perspiration flowed from every pore, so great was the inner heat and the intensity of my prayer. After awhile, the force subsided and I was left feeling relaxed and serene. A great calm pervaded my being and I felt an inner assurance; I was no longer concerned about my physical condition, no longer anxious about the near or distant future.

I was permitted to complete the senior year of school studies by writing weekly reports and taking the required examinations at home. In early summer, I was able to leave my bed and slowly begin the return to normal activities. The day I stood before the mirror for the first time in five months, I was shocked by what I saw. A little over six feet in height, I weighed only one hundred and twenty-five pounds! I had lost forty-five pounds of body weight during my illness. But the pain was gone, and the high fevers I had once experienced were now a thing of the past. A new surge of vitality was springing forth from inner sources. Even so, for the first few days, to walk from room to room required that I hold onto something for support—a door frame, a chair, or a helping arm.

It was in the evening of the first day of my convalescence that my mother made her transition from the body. She had nursed me with loving attention from the beginning of my illness. She had planned, when I was again healthy, to take a short vacation, to rest and to visit relatives.

That evening, I had been lightly sleeping when I heard my father call to me. Making my way slowly to the back door, I peered out into the darkness. "Son," my father cried, "Your mother has had an accident. I'm going to the neighbor's house to call the doctor!" When the doctor arrived twenty minutes later, he pronounced my mother dead of a heart attack. She was forty-six years of age.

A few minutes before she passed she had been sitting on the porch, in a swing. My father was at the kitchen sink, preparing for bed. My mother called to him, telling him that she was having difficulty breathing. My father hastened to her side and helped her down the cement steps to the lawn, so she could recline and relax. Her last words were to my father, as he held her in his arms. She looked at him and said, "Oh, hon, I'm going to die!" Then she was gone. My father later told me that at the moment of her transition he saw a light come from her face.

My mother's body was buried in a small cemetery at Braceville, Ohio, near the black community where so many of my school friends lived. Because of my own recent experience of serious illness, during which I had often deeply contemplated the subject of death, I felt no deep grief, no sense of real loss, when my mother left us. I had already seen the larger plan, and was able to accept life's changes as part of that plan.

Once, while helping my father repair a piece of farm equipment, he shared with me an experience he had had when he was a young man. He began by saying, "Son, don't ever say anything bad about anyone, because sometimes what you say about them can come true."

He continued, "Years ago, when I was still courting your mother, the old car I was driving had a flat tire and I pulled off to the side of the road to repair it. I was a little bit angry about the situation and, while I was working on the tire, a car came by and the driver laughed and made an unkind remark. I said to myself, 'Darn you. I hope you have *four* flat tires today!'" Father paused for a few moments, then said, "You know, after I got that tire fixed and started down the road, we finally saw that man and that car parked off the road and all four tires were flat! I believe to this day that my words made it happen, and it still bothers me. So, son, never say anything bad about anyone, especially if you're angry."

After a longer pause, he said, "I really believe there are things in this world that we don't understand, and we have to be careful about what we say and do."

In casual conversations with me, father would occasionally share his feelings about matters which were seldom otherwise discussed. It was as though we shared an inner understanding which did not require extensive explanations. He loved the land and all things natural, and was a quiet individualist in many ways. His grandfather on his mother's side of the family was American Indian—which tribe is not known. His father came to this country from Wales; the Welsh are reputed to be gifted with "second sight" or psychic abilities.

Through the summer and early autumn months of 1949 I maintained a regular schedule of meditation, asanas and sunbathing, while continuing my self-prescribed vegetarian diet. Recovery was rapid, and the doctor, when he visited on random occasions, was pleasantly amazed. During these months my father attended to farm chores and hauled coal for customers. I looked after my five-year-old sister, who was the only child other than myself left at home, and prepared the meals for the family. It was in late November of that year that I left home.

TWO

I Meet My Guru,
Paramahansa Yogananda

With a bus ticket, some clothes in a suitcase, and a little less than one hundred dollars in my pocket, I traveled to Miami, Florida. My plan was to avoid another winter season in Ohio and to earn enough money in Florida to go to California. The bus trip was a novel experience for me; until then, I had not traveled more than two hundred miles from the place of my birth.

After renting a room for two dollars a day in a modest hotel in Miami, I found employment as a food preparer in a small restaurant which catered mainly to breakfast and lunch customers. My pay was one dollar per hour, plus a noon meal. After several days at the job, it became obvious to me that saving money for travel in this way would be an almost impossible process, so I signed on as part of a group of young men who were hired to sell magazine subscriptions from door to door.

One day during this period, an interesting encounter took place in West Palm Beach. When I knocked on the door of an older house in the suburbs, a pleasant woman opened the door and greeted me. She didn't buy any magazines from me, but she did invite me into her home for a light snack. While we were talking, she asked about my plans for the future. Without hesitation I informed her that I was going to California to study with Paramahansa Yogananda.

Showing no surprise, she led me to her library. There, on neatly arranged shelves, I saw hundreds of books on every aspect of spiritual science. She informed me that it was "in this very room" that William Walker Atkinson had, years earlier, written many of his books. Atkinson was a prolific author in the early decades of this century. Under his own name, he wrote books on mental science and New Thought themes. Under his pen name, Yogi Ramacharaka, he wrote books explaining the practices of yoga.

I thanked my hostess and prepared to leave. At the door, as we were saying goodbye, she suggested that perhaps I might want to consider going to California immediately, instead of remaining with the sales crew.

I thought about it, and that evening, when the sales crew drove to Tampa, I told the crew manager that I felt I should leave. The next morning, he drove me to the edge of the city and gave me five dollars in exchange for my wristwatch as security. I redeemed the watch from him a few weeks later by sending the money from California.

That morning, I purchased some nuts, raisins and oatmeal at a convenience store, to ensure that I would have something to eat along the way. Standing by the side of the road, I held out my arm, thumb raised, to flag approaching motorists. No ride was offered that first day, and the night was spent huddled over a small wood fire which I made in a nearby orange grove.

The next day, armed with a positive mental attitude, I was given a ride to Tallahassee, and then on to De Funiak Springs, where I was allowed to spend the night in the office of a service station. Early the next morning before sunrise, a black man stopped for gasoline and offered to take me as far as Pensacola. There, while I was standing in the lightly falling rain, the owner of a nearby restaurant called out to me.

"Hey, son, come on in out of the rain!" He held the door open in welcome as he waved to me.

Once I was inside, he insisted on serving me a substantial breakfast and said, "It's on the house. Good luck on the road." When the rain abated I again flagged the passing cars. I decided to make a game of it. I would say to myself, "One of the next six cars will stop for me." Five cars passed. The sixth also went by without stopping. Then, in the distance, I saw the car stop, turn around and come back to where I stood. A young couple, with much luggage in the car, offered to take me to New Orleans.

After we had been driving a few minutes the young woman said, "You may not believe this, but it's true. After we passed you back there we both looked at each other and said, "Let's go back and offer him a ride."

So the journey of faith went, from New Orleans to Houston, and on to El Paso, Tucson, and Riverside, California. In Riverside I slept in a bed for the first time in six days. When I had arrived at the Salvation Army hostel in Riverside, the evening meal had not yet been served. I was made welcome, and asked to sweep the front steps and sidewalk in front of the building.

In the morning, after breakfast, I was given a ride to downtown Los Angeles, where I immediately asked for directions to the public library. There, I was astounded to see a vast room, one of many in the library, housing thousands of volumes on religion and philosophy. I found back issues of *Self-Realization Magazine* and noted the exact address of the headquarters in the Highland Park district of the city.

That afternoon was spent in reading as many issues of the magazine as I could, in order to more familiarize myself with the organization. At dusk a helpful person directed me to the Fifth Street Mission, a few blocks away. There I was provided with a meal and a clean bed in the dormitory.

Returning to the library the next morning, I read from *Autobiography of a Yogi* and wondered what my reception would be like when I went to SRF headquarters. Then, in the late afternoon, carrying my suitcase, I walked to a main street and asked the clerk in a corner store for directions. He provided explicit instructions and even offered streetcar fare, which I

Paramahansa Yogananda, 1949, Los Angeles, California.

gratefully accepted—my original five dollars had already been spent.

A week earlier, when beginning the westward trek, I had inwardly resolved not to ask for anything except transportation along the way. Yet, without my asking, I was always provided with regular meals and shelter at night was always somehow available. I had faith that God was with me and frequent evidence of His caring deepened that faith.

As a child I discovered that if I really wanted anything, if I could visualize it and feel that I possessed it, it would come into my life. Many people use this creative process without ever connecting effects with the cause. Since the human mind is a portion of a universal mind, whatever we vividly visualize and believe in tends to unfold on the screen of space.

Getting off the streetcar at the bottom of Mt. Washington, I began to wend my way up the steep drive. A passing car stopped and the driver asked, "Where are you going?" When I told him, he said, "Get in; I'll take you right to the front gate."

A cottage stood to the left, just inside the main entrance of the ten-acre estate. Ralph Sherman, a resident disciple, responded to my knock on the door. We talked for a minute, and he took me to the men's dining room, where several monks were gathered for their evening meal. I was invited to join them.

Most of them were young, a few about my age and several in their mid-twenties. Donald Walters, who was later to become Swami Kriyananda and found the Ananda Community near Nevada City, California, introduced himself and invited me to join him for a talk after the meal, in the main room on the first floor of the building.

Once we were settled in the spacious and well-appointed room, Donald asked me about myself, my intentions, the reason for my being there, and other matters. He was very polite and cheerful, and made me feel comfortable and at home.

As we were talking, we heard the sound of an elevator descending. Donald stood up and with a happy smile exclaimed,

"Master is coming!" Following his lead I stood and turned toward the hallway entrance.

Paramahansaji came into the room. He was wearing a dark blue suit and overcoat, a white neck scarf and a felt hat. He was dressed to go out, and his car was waiting at the bottom of the porch steps a few yards away. He acknowledged Donald, then looked directly into my eyes. I will never forget that look: beautiful brown eyes that shared fathomless love and revealed a soul anchored in the Infinite.

He smiled gently and shook my hand. His first words to me were, "How old are you?"

"Eighteen, sir," I replied.

"Do your parents know you've come here?" was his second question.

"It's all right, sir," I assured him.

Paramahansaji continued to look into my eyes. Then, with a touch of his right hand on my forehead, he murmured, "I'll see you again." He then proceeded, with a few women disciples, to walk to his car and was driven off into the night.

It was Paramahansaji's habit to bless disciples by touching them lightly at the spiritual eye center. In this way a guru shares his consciousness and vital force, so that the energies of the disciple are quickened.

After Master left, Donald led me along a garden path to a dormitory building, where the resident monks were getting settled for the night. A few were practicing yogasanas on the floor; some were meditating quietly. The room was crowded because of the many visitors who had arrived to attend the weekend programs. The next day, Saturday, was Christmas Eve and the occasion of an all-day meditation conducted by Paramahansaji. On Christmas Day there was to be a banquet in the late afternoon.

So it was that I arrived at my guru's home on the 23rd of December, 1949. It was the beginning of almost four years as a monk of the Self-Realization Fellowship.

By mid-morning of Christmas Eve day two hundred or more disciples and students were gathered in the lower room of the main building, awaiting Paramahansaji's arrival. The program was delayed for an hour or so because he had not yet come down. During this interlude I was introduced to the rest of the monks, those whom I had not met the evening before. When Master finally arrived, he entered the room slowly, escorted by his most advanced male disciple, Mr. J. J. Lynn, whom all referred to as "St. Lynn." Mr. Lynn was later to be given the monastic name of Rajarsi Janakananda and would, in 1952, succeed Paramahansaji as President and spiritual head of the movement. They were both radiant, and a profound aura of peace and God consciousness enveloped them as they came into the room. Walking slowly to the front of the chapel, they sat side by side on chairs which had been placed before the altar. The rest of us then entered the chapel and were seated.

Framed photographs of Babaji, Lahiri Mahasaya, Swami Sri Yukteswar and Paramahansaji adorned the altar, along with a representative portrait of Jesus. Candles were lighted and the fragrance of incense wafted through the chapel.

Master began talking, slowly, speaking the names of beloved disciples and gently emphasizing the importance of loving God. He spoke of God as one who knew Him, and he spoke of God as the Divine Mother. God as father is the aspect of the Godhead which is beyond creation, and causes its manifestation. God as mother is the divine energy expressing as creation. It was a magical experience for me to be with so many devotees of God and to be able to see, before me, my spiritual master.

Paramahansaji spoke reverently of Christ and of the guru line. The quiet but dynamic spiritual power in the room was electric. Even without meditating, one could sit and absorb the purity and heavenly joy of the moment.

Dr. M. W. Lewis, visiting from Boston, sat at the organ and began, at a signal from Master, to play one of the beautiful devotional chants which Master had adapted from the Indian original. Master's vibrant voice led us in song. He said, before we began to chant, "Chanting is half the battle in meditation. When you chant with love for God, until all stray thoughts are driven from the mind, then you will experience His presence."

Rajarsi Janakananda (Mr. J.J. Lynn)

When the final refrains faded into silence, Master instructed us in meditation procedure, and we then sat in the silence.

Over the many years that I have been ministering I have often been told that when I lead a group meditation something special occurs. I know this to be true, because I also experience it. There is something that many do not know; I learned how to meditate, and how to lead meditation, from a perfect master of yoga.

From time to time during the Christmas Eve meditation that day, Master asked us to stand while chanting, to afford us an opportunity for body movement so that we would be more comfortable when we again sat to meditate. Among the several chants were, "O God Beautiful," "In the Temple of Silence," and "Who is in My Temple?" All were simple melodies, with key stanzas repeated several times.

After about three hours, a short rest break was announced. One monk told me later that, as he left the chapel, he had *felt* several strong gusts of wind pass him in the hall. When he returned to the chapel Paramahansaji asked him, with joy in his voice, "Did you see them? Did you see them? There were saints who left this room when you did!"

I was later to learn that Paramahansaji would, at times, speak of the saints and masters who visited him in their subtle forms. Spiritually advanced souls, who are free to move through the veils which bar ordinary mortals, are often drawn to earthly shrines and sacred places where love for God is evident.

During the afternoon session, while Paramahansaji spoke of Krishna and Radha, Spirit and Nature, Mr. Lynn suddenly slumped in his chair. Before long he regained his composure and resumed his upright meditation posture, tears of bliss streaming from his eyes. Paramahansaji chuckled softly and remarked, "St. Lynn can't stand it when I talk like this. He always goes into ecstasy!"

When the meditation was concluded, Master stood at the doorway and blessed each person as he or she departed.

I attended the Hollywood Self-Realization Church of All Religions the next morning. Master conducted the service, reading selections from *The New Testament* and *The Bhagavad Gita.* After leading us in meditation, he delivered the sermon-lesson. His presentation was unique. He wove a spell of love as he talked, sometimes of intimate and personal matters; at other times he was the powerful orator. He made frequent use of anecdotes, and his occasional interjection of humor enlivened his presentation and bound the congregation closer to him.

After the benediction, one of the sisters of the Order approached me and said, "Master wants to see you later, when he has seen all the others who have been scheduled for interviews."

At that time, it was Paramahansaji's custom to meet with students and friends after the Sunday morning service, and it was often late in the afternoon before he departed for Mt. Washington.

When I was finally summoned I was led to a small room, just to the left of the stage. Master was there, sitting on a couch, and as I entered he motioned for me to sit beside him. I was awed by the pervasive aura of love and power. He put me at ease with his gentle gaze and friendly smile. Nothing was said for a moment. Then he asked, his words barely audible, "What can I do for you?"

His eyes danced with merriment, because he knew why I was there, but he wanted me to verbalize my purpose. I responded, "I want to be your disciple, sir." He seemed pleased at my forthright statement, then said, "This is not a path of escapism, you know."

"How is your health?" the next question came. He knew of my illness earlier that year. It might have been a routine question, but his probing gaze hinted at more than that. When I told him that I felt well, he reached out his left hand and felt my pulse, at the wrist, and was quiet for a moment. Then he smiled and reassured me, "Yes, you are all right now."

Those who are trained in Ayurveda, the Science of Life, know how to discern the total condition of the physical body by feeling the pulse. One who is skilled in the procedure can detect, through touch alone, the vitality of the patient and the condition of all major systems and organs.

After a few more exchanges, he touched me at the spiritual eye and said, "You stay; I'll see you from time to time."

That evening many friends and disciples gathered in the main room of Mt. Washington headquarters for the annual Christmas banquet. Everyone was standing, awaiting Master's arrival. St. Lynn entered through a side door, chatting with a few male disciples, and joined us. When I was introduced to him he graciously acknowledged me and shared a few private words of wisdom.

"Everything is God's grace and Master's love," he said. "Meditate every day, in the beginning, if only for fifteen to twenty minutes at a time. After awhile it will become a habit and good things will happen."

When Master entered the room the assembled friends and disciples took their seats at the long tables, and bowls and platters of food were brought from the central kitchen. The meal was splendid! Varied dishes were offered: curried vegetables, rice, breads and salads, several Indian dishes which were new to me and, of course, dessert. Master, sitting at the head table with older disciples and invited friends, would occasionally speak to us of God's love and of his own love for us.

The next several weeks were spent doing whatever I was asked to do by the senior monks. Sometimes I assisted in raking leaves from the lawn, and sweeping the lower halls of the building. For a brief duration I typed form letters, sent to persons who were receiving the weekly lessons. Donald Walters was then supervising that department.

Several days were spent at the SRF Lake Shrine in Pacific Palisades. This then newly acquired property was opened to the public and dedicated on August 20, 1950. Surrounding a small lake are shrines and meditation nooks. Tall towers, topped with gold-leafed copper lotus buds, serve as a central focus. Behind them, a few yards distant, stands an ancient Chinese stone sarcophagus, ornately carved, in which were placed during the dedication ceremonies a portion of the ashes

of Mahatma Gandhi, which a friend of Paramahansaji had sent
from India.

Except for weekends and holidays the daily routine at Mt.
Washington was fixed. We would assemble on the tennis court
at 6:30 each morning, to practice the special energization exercises which Paramahansaji had devised decades earlier. These
exercises consist of mild muscular tension along with a special
breathing process, with some movement of the limbs, while
one visualizes life force flowing from the medulla oblongata
to the body part being exercised. Yogis teach that soul force
enters the body at the medulla. Paramahansaji taught these
exercises as a way to consciously vitalize the body with this
force.

After the exercise period we assembled in the chapel for a
thirty-minute meditation, after which we went to breakfast.
Following breakfast, we were given our work assignments for
the day. In the evening, another exercise and meditation period was observed from 5 P.M. until 6 P.M., before the evening
meal. The remaining hours until bedtime were designated as
free time, during which some disciples studied, meditated, or
practiced yogasanas. Those new to the ashram then had an
opportunity to learn from senior disciples who would instruct
in Hatha Yoga procedures or conduct discussion groups.

From time to time, when Paramahansaji would enjoy a
quiet stroll on the grounds of Mt. Washington and we would
be fortunate enough to happen upon him, he would pause for
a while and talk with us. It was during these unplanned occasions that we were allowed to share the intimate and personal
side of our guru, as he told anecdotes, gave instructions on
practical and spiritual matters, and revealed his personal interest in us.

He would often say, "I go through your souls every day. I
keep track of you and I am able to help you, if you will allow
me to help you."

With increasing frequency, whenever we would meet, he
would say, "Be patient, Roy; I have plans for you." At this
time, he had not yet formally accepted me as a disciple, al-

though he treated me as one and expected me to conduct myself accordingly.

I had been assigned a corner area in the men's dormitory for my private use. There I read, meditated, and slept. On weekends I would seek out a quiet place on the grounds and meditate for longer periods of time, sometimes alone and on occasion with a few of the other monks. I never discussed my inner perceptions with others, not even with Master unless he asked me, which he seldom did. He never had to ask about a disciple's inner condition because he possessed insight which enabled him to know anything he wanted to know. Later I was also able to know by knowing, an ability which unfolded with time and not one which required effort to develop.

As the months passed I experienced direct transmission of knowledge through my guru. When I was with him I could discern his moods and his thoughts, and when I was not in his presence I could be "with him" soul to soul. On many occasions when I would discern his unspoken thoughts, he would turn to me and share a knowing smile.

THREE

Discipleship and Experiences on the Path

It was late one afternoon when the work crew completed the pouring of the concrete lower walls of India House. This facility had been designed to accommodate the overflow attendance from the adjacent Hollywood SRF church, and to provide space for a project of Master's—a vegetarian menu restaurant. The contractor and his men were leaving at the end of the work day, and we monks were cleaning tools, preparatory to driving back to Mt. Washington. Reverend Bernard, a senior monk, arrived to inspect the work and, seeing me, waved me over to where he stood.

"Master wants to see you tonight," he said. "Be downstairs near the men's kitchen at seven o'clock. He is going to the desert retreat tonight and will be gone for several months. He wants to see you before he goes."

Paramahansaji was then arranging the closing years of his earth stay. He had given his last Sunday morning talk at the Hollywood church and was planning to live in seclusion, in a small house which had been purchased near Twenty-Nine Palms, California. There he would finish his updated commentary on *The Bhagavad Gita*, as well as commentaries on the

Book of Genesis and *The New Testament*. I was later to occasionally visit him there.

Upon returning to Mt. Washington with the other monks, I quickly bathed, attended the group meditation, and joined the others in the kitchen for the evening meal. "Why does he want to see me?" the thought arose in my mind. I was inwardly joyful at the opportunity to be with him again.

The men's kitchen was located in the basement of the main building on the grounds. When the others departed after supper I was left alone to wait in the basement hallway. I sat quietly, meditating and inwardly chanting the names of God and the guru line. As I write now, it seems only yesterday that these events unfolded, so vivid is the memory. I felt that an important moment in my life was about to be experienced, and I awaited Master's arrival in a state of keen anticipation.

I waited. I kept on waiting. Only silence—not a person stirred; no sounds came from outside to disturb my solitude. I was physically tired, but mentally alert. Finally, sometime before midnight, I decided that there had been a communications lag and retired to the men's dormitory to sleep.

The next morning a brother monk approached me and asked, "Where were you last night? Master returned about midnight, and the first thing he said was, 'Where's Roy?' I replied, 'I think he went to bed. I'll go get him.' Master said, 'It's all right; I'll see him tomorrow.'"

I was crestfallen and ashamed at my lack of patience. Then, later in the day Reverend Bernard spoke to me, and with a smile said, "Master wants to see you tonight. Same place, same time."

I was there promptly at seven. At about nine o'clock, there was a sudden flurry of activity as Master's car was brought to the entrance of the building and disciples began to bring down luggage. Male and female disciples lined the hall to bid him farewell. After a while, word was passed along that Master was talking by telephone to a disciple in the midwest and would not be leaving until the next morning. The disciples melted into the night, the car was returned to the garage, and I was again

Swami Sri Yukteswar, guru of Paramahansa Yogananda.

left alone; I was inwardly committed not to move from the spot, and to sit there through the night, if need be.

Soon, I heard the elevator slowly descend. The door slid open, and Master peered out. When he saw me standing there, he smiled and exclaimed, "There's my boy!"

Gesturing for me to follow him, Master walked a few yards down the hall to Reverend Bernard's apartment and there knocked loudly on the door, punctuating the knocks with a commanding, "Bernard, Bernard, let me in!"

The door was quickly opened and Master entered the room. I followed behind him. Another disciple was also there. Master was dressed to walk in the night air, and was munching from a handful of almonds. Catching my eye, he said, smiling, "This is the first thing I've had to eat all day."

He motioned for me to stand before him. Taking my right hand with his own, he instructed, "Kneel down, Roy." I knelt before him, our hands clasped.

"When my guru, Sri Yukteswar, accepted me," he began, "he said, 'I promise you my unconditional love. No matter what you do, or fail to do, I will love you eternally.'" Master paused, then continued, "I promise you my unconditional love. No matter what you do, or fail to do, I will love you eternally. Can you pledge this same love for me?"

I responded, "Yes, sir." He then blessed me by touching my head and had me stand up. Looking deep into my eyes, he said, "Will you do what I ask you to do?"

"Yes, sir."

"I want you to go to Phoenix. Bernard will take you to the train station in the morning. We have a new project there and I want you to be part of it. The climate will be good for your health, too."

After a brief planning discussion with Bernard, Master again blessed me and left for his walk; I went to the men's dorm to sleep.

The "new project" in Arizona was a goat dairy, recently purchased by the organization as a business venture, as well as a training environment for male monastics. Since I had grown up working on the family farm in Ohio. and knew how to work

with farm animals, it would be a somewhat familiar environment for me.

Early the next morning I was enroute to Arizona by train,
arriving late in the afternoon. Reverend Bernard's mother, Mrs.
Cole, was then living at the SRF Phoenix Center; the minister
there, Herbert Freed, lived in a small room attached to the
garage. Mrs. Cole had a meal prepared for me, and soon Herbert arrived and we became acquainted. He immediately began
to launch into a detailed explanation of the superiority of
goat's milk over cow's milk and painted a vivid mental picture
of what a glorious success the dairy was going to be!

The site of the Rosebud Goat Dairy was a five-acre plot
less than three miles from the heart of Scottsdale, about a
twenty-minute drive from the center in Phoenix. For a modest
sum, the organization had obtained the five acres, two dozen
goats, a small house, a building for processing the milk, and a
wooden barn. This was to be my "monastery" for the next
year.

We would awake at dawn, meditate, and then milk and
feed the goats. The milk was bottled and loaded onto the
truck, and Herbert would drive off to deliver it to customers.
My job was to clean the barn, sweep the pens and, from time
to time, irrigate the pasture. At night, in my private room, I
would meditate long and deep.

My meditation procedure at this time was as follows: I
would sit before a small altar upon which photographs of
Babaji, Lahiri, Sri Yukteswar and Master had been placed. A
print of an artist's conception of Jesus was also on the altar.
I would pray to God and ask my guru line to infuse me with
their consciousness. Then I would chant some of the devotional chants which Paramahansaji had adapted to English.
Becoming more interiorized, I would practice the hong-sau
mantra, letting the mantra float in the mind, synchronized
with natural breathing rhythm. Gradually the mantra would
recede and I would surrender to the third eye center or the
crown chakra, listening to the inner sound.

One night I had a vivid experience, surprising yet revealing. While resting in the silence, after having practiced

various meditation techniques, I suddenly found myself to be a point of awareness, located at the sacral chakra. I could see inside my body; all of the organs were bathed in white light. It seemed a most natural perception. Then, I felt myself "growing" until I again filled the body.

Master had counseled me earlier, "Stay in tune with me and I will be able to help you. When you are restless, or filled with doubts, this causes static in the mental radio and makes it harder for me to help you. So stay in tune with me."

As the months unfolded I found that it was indeed true that Master knew my thoughts and feelings, even though we were hundreds of miles apart. When I experienced a duration of apathy, he would write a brief note and have it mailed to me. Invariably, his words proved that he knew exactly what my inner condition was.

I occasionally experienced periods of moodiness, feeling that God would never respond to my prayers, or that the road to liberation was too long and arduous. During one of these phases Master sent a note in which he advised, "Roy, you make yourself unhappy by constantly replaying the old mental phonograph record. Why don't you just break the record?" That, and his grace, were all I needed to banish the habit of moody self-indulgence.

When it became obvious that the goat dairy would not prosper because of the small volume of milk we were able to market, it was decided that more goats should be purchased. In a few weeks, two large trucks arrived and about eighty goats were unloaded. Now we had the potential! We also had to build two more barns to house them during the rainy season and the cold winter nights to come.

Two more monks were assigned to the dairy. One of them, Leo Cocks, remains a close friend and brother to this day. We built the barns by laying adobe bricks. We planned the breeding schedule so that we would have an average of forty goats at peak milking condition the year around. Before long we were producing more milk than we could successfully market. We now had the product, but we didn't have the marketing skills to get the product to the consumers.

We decided to use the excess milk to make cheese. We didn't know how to market that, either, and we became increasingly frustrated with the situation. Herbert became more and more anxious, because he felt that Master was depending upon him to make the business a success. A year or so after the project began, it was decided that the dairy should be sold. Many years later, while visiting Phoenix, I drove to Scottsdale to find the site of the former dairy. No evidence of it remains, so extensive has the growth been in the Scottsdale area.

During that first year I had the opportunity to visit Master on several occasions. He had instructed me to visit him in California at least every two months. An interesting incident took place during one of these visits to him.

I had gone to Twenty-Nine Palms and was taken to a cottage located a few miles from where Master was living. During the days I would be at his retreat, working on the grounds. Late one morning Master came out to inspect the improvements currently being made on the garage. An older disciple was nailing wire onto the garage walls in preparation for stucco coating. Master said to him, "Jerry, get the pump and start draining the swimming pool."

To my utter surprise, Jerry didn't even look up when Master addressed him. He retorted, "I can't do it now, sir, I'm busy with this job." I couldn't believe that a disciple could talk like that to his guru.

Master turned to me and asked, "Will you empty the pool, Roy?" I agreed. He told me that I would find two five-gallon buckets in the garage; I was to use them to bail the water from the swimming pool.

Attaching a rope to one bucket, I would drop it into the pool, recover it, and then pour the contents into the other bucket. Then, refilling the first bucket with water from the pool, I would carry both of them to the nearby desert plants and pour out the water.

It was a small pool, but it contained many thousands of gallons of water. For the rest of that day, I carried water from the pool to plants and shrubs all over the grounds. My hands were raw, my muscles ached, perspiration was profuse, but I never thought of quitting. At midday, one of Master's secretaries brought me a pair of gloves, and by the end of the day the water line had dropped by at least three feet, but there were still many hundreds of gallons of water remaining.

The next day when Master came out, from his vantage point near the house the pool appeared to be empty. He exclaimed, "My God! Look what Roy has done!" Coming closer, he saw the remaining water in the pool. He didn't even look around for Jerry; he simply raised his voice and shouted, "Jerry, get the pump!" Jerry got the pump.

The most enjoyable moments, during those visits in the desert, were the evenings when Master would take a stroll around the circumference of the property and invite me to walk with him. Now and then, during these walks, he would notice a scrap of paper on the ground and ask me to remove it. Sometimes we walked in silence, holding hands as we went. Sometimes he would spot a small stone and kick it a few feet ahead, playing like a child. Sometimes he would look at the nearby mountains.

On one such occasion he said to me, "You know, most people, when they see that mountain, see only a mass of earth and rocks. When I look at it, I see only God."

An amusing, yet transforming incident occurred during one visit to the desert retreat. For several days prior to going to visit Master, I had been experiencing mild but sharp shooting pains in my chest and left arm, usually in the evenings after a hard day's work. I wondered if I were straining my body. Also, because of my history of rheumatic fever, I wondered if my heart could be malfunctioning.

When I first saw Master on that visit, we met on the patio near his house. He inquired, "How are your parents?" My mind interpreted his question differently. When he had gotten as far as, "How are your pa. . ." my mind assumed that he had said, "How is your pain?" Talk about self-centeredness! So I responded, "It's not too bad now, sir."

Master looked at me inquiringly and asked, "What's not bad now?" I said, "This pain I've been having."

"You have a pain?"

As I began to describe it, he dismissed my recital with a simple statement. Touching me lightly on the chest, he said, "It'll be all right." Then he changed the subject. I never had another pain of that nature.

On one occasion, a few monks were eating lunch on the patio, and Master came out to visit with us. He had been fasting, but he insisted that we eat well. Noticing a soybean food product on one of the monks' plates, he asked permission to sample it. The plate was proffered and Master took a small bite, chewed it a few times and then spat out the remains on the ground. With a mischievous smile and a wink of the eye he confided to us, "I'm on a fast. You all saw me. . .I didn't eat it!"

During my first visit with Master I had occasion to experience how he was able to make his point with disciples who were in need of instruction. The hour was late, the sun had gone down hours earlier, and the few monks present were about to drive back to the cottage. Master had been walking, carrying a flashlight. A few female monastics were also present as we all gathered about Master near the gate.

After talking quietly with us for several minutes he directed the beam from his flashlight into my face and held it steady. Then, very gently, he said for all to hear, "Roy, do you remember when you first came to me?" I responded in the affirmative. He continued, "Well, I asked some of these people if I should keep you or not. Do you know what they said?"

"No, sir," I replied. Master explained. "When you came to me I asked them, 'Shall we let him stay?' They said, 'He was sick; maybe he'll get sick again.'"

He paused. There were a few moments of absolute silence. Everyone knew he was making a point. He then resumed, "But I looked into your heart, and I said, 'He stays.'" Another pause. His final words that evening were, "Good night, Roy." With that he turned and walked towards the house. No one else said anything for a long time.

Paramahansaji, being a guru in the tradition of the *siddhas*, the perfect masters, could read the inner karma and the destiny of souls. He used to say, "I am not interested in an organization merely for the sake of having an organization. An organization of this nature, without the honey of God, is of no value at all. I am interested only in souls."

A few weeks after my initial arrival at Mt. Washington, and before being accepted by Master as a disciple, I began to experience surprising energy movements in the spine. When I would pause while at work, to rest a few moments, a strong surge of electric force would ascend the spinal pathway, causing the body to involuntarily jerk and twitch; the major sensation was in the spine and brain. This would also happen when I sat to meditate.

A brother disciple noticed this body movement on one occasion and asked me about it. When I explained the symptoms he laughed and said, "Oh, that's because you're seeing Master now and then, and because you're in his environment."

I did not know it at the time, but I had received *shaktipat*, the transmission of spiritual force from the guru to the receptive disciple. Part of the transformation process, when one comes into contact with his guru, is that the dormant spiritual energies are aroused so that they can be utilized in one's spiritual practices. This force which flows from guru to disciple can flow spontaneously when the disciple is receptive to it. The guru can also transmit it through touch, through the gaze, and through an act of will. I had not anticipated the experience, so it came as a complete surprise to me.

I found, with experience, that if I relaxed, the energy would surge strongly, but that there would be no involuntary body movements. Instead, the inner experience was more ecstatic because the currents were being allowed to flow through deeper channels, instead of being drained off through muscular spasms.

Later, I was to observe Master carefully looking at a disciple from time to time. He was looking for signs of that person's inner condition. I know, from my own experience with him, that he could accurately discern a disciple's inner condition by looking into the eyes. He could also do it by merely thinking of the disciple, if the disciple was absent.

Whenever I would visit him he would look at me. If I had

been having calm meditations and my life was well ordered, he would exclaim, "Look at how calm and God-loving you are becoming! Continue doing what you are doing." If I was not as centered as I would have liked to have been, he would look at me and say, "You must meditate more, Roy. Dive deep into the ocean of God. Pray to God and tell Him, 'Lord, I want nothing but You, only You.'"

During that first year I experienced God's grace in a very personal way. The occasion was the dedication of the SRF Lake Shrine. One of my fantasies was that, if I were prepared, Master would touch me at the spiritual eye and transmit his consciousness to me and I would transcend mental conditioning and experience samadhi. For several weeks before the dedication of the Lake Shrine, I deliberately maintained a positive mental outlook, meditated deeply, talked very little, and ate very little. I wanted my nervous system to be attuned and my soul nature responsive.

Sitting in the back seat of the bus, traveling all night from Phoenix to Los Angeles to attend the dedication ceremonies, I slept very little. When not dozing I meditated and practiced kriya pranayamas. I just "knew" that Master would see that I was ready for the great experience!

Upon arriving at Mt. Washington, I was greeted by my fellow monks and told the schedule for the day. The long-anticipated dedication of the Lake Shrine was a great success! Hundreds of people were there. The Lieutenant Governor of the State of California, Goodwin Knight, addressed the assemblage, and other notables participated. Master delivered a stirring address to the assembled crowd. Then a few monks demonstrated hatha yoga poses, after which everyone was invited to form a line and pass by Master's chair in order to have a word with him and to receive his blessing.

I waited until almost everyone had had a chance to spend a few moments with Master, then approached him. He touched me at the spiritual eye and asked how I had been. I leaned close, to speak to him in confidence. He inclined his head and turned his ear to me. I said just the words, "Sir, will you give me samadhi?" He looked at me with an amused smile. "What

did you say?" he inquired. I repeated my request. He chuckled
and grasped me by my hair, giving my head a loving shake.
Still holding me by the hair with his left hand, he turned to St.
Lynn, who was sitting in meditation to his right, and tapped
him on the knee. "He wants samadhi," Master said. They both
smiled broadly. Then St. Lynn said softly, "Bless his heart."

With a gesture of blessing, Master moved me through the
line. It had been such a happy, spontaneous, loving encounter
that I could not feel disappointment. After all, at the time I
wasn't even really conscious of what it was I was asking for.

A short time later that same day, I was standing alone by
the path near the Lake, when I saw St. Lynn walking in my
direction. I held my hands together in a gesture of respect,
assuming that he would continue on past me. Instead, he
stopped in front of me, closed his eyes, placed his left hand
over my heart and his right hand on my head. He rocked me
back and forth gently, to induce relaxation. Suddenly, I felt a
stream of liquid energy flow into the heart chakra and I began
to expand, until my awareness extended beyond the confines
of the physical form.

I experienced indescribable joy, bliss, love, purity, and ex-
panded awareness, all simultaneously. When I was filled, and
overflowing, St. Lynn stepped back, smiled sweetly, and
walked on to where Master was sitting.

I remained rooted to the spot, motionless for a duration.
Then, gradually, the mind began to work. It thought, "There's
a small cabin on the hill overlooking the shrine area. If I can
get up there, away from the possible disturbance of people
here, this experience can continue to completion."

So much for thinking! I should have just sat down where I
was; no one would have thought it unusual for a monk. Instead, I ran up the path to the crest of the hill. By the time I
arrived at my destination I was breathing so hard that I was
more body-conscious than soul-conscious.

However, the subtle inner change remained permanent. To
this day, I can experience a similar perception, merely by
thinking about the incident. A Zen proverb states, "One can
never experience anything again; one can only recall it." This

is true. It is also true that by vividly recalling an experience to mind, one can experience a currently fresh, similar experience.

I noticed, when with Master, that he would share with a disciple according to that disciple's capacity to receive. With me, he always talked of God, and the masters; of life's true purpose, and of the importance of steadiness and dedication on the path. He enlivened my soul capacities. He enriched my mind. He reinforced my faith. He told me I was meant to be with him and that my future was wonderful.

A few days after my first Christmas with him, in 1949, I was in the lower hallway when Master came through. He had arranged for the purchase of a ping-pong ball set for the use of the monks, as his token Christmas present to them. At first, the game was set up on the front porch, just under the windows of Master's room, but the noise caused by various enthusiastic players had resulted in the table and materials being moved to the lower hallway. That night, he saw the table and motioned for me to pick up a paddle and hit the ball to him. We batted it back and forth a few times. Suddenly, he "slammed" the ball and scored the point. Putting the paddle down, he turned to those with him (Sister Dayamata, her sister, and one or two others) and asked, "Who used to be the champion ping-pong ball player here?" They smiled at their memories.

Walking to the elevator, Master and the others entered it. Before the door closed he looked out, straight into my eyes, and said, "You have a wonderful future, Roy." He held my gaze for just a brief moment, then said, "Good night, Roy."

I remember another occasion when Master was returning from an errand and invited himself into the men's kitchen. A few of us sat around the table with him, delighted that he wanted to share his private time with us. He asked if we had any food readily available. Someone found a box of Post Toasties, a ready-to-eat flaked cereal, and some milk. A bowl was provided, and Master enjoyed his snack, all the while talking with us.

Suddenly, he spotted a bottle of hot sauce. "Let me have that," he demanded. It was passed to him. He removed the cap, poured a liberal quantity of the hot mixture into a spoon and swallowed it with seeming enthusiasm! Then, pouring a small quantity into the spoon, he instructed, "Line up, boys; you're in for an experience!"

We lined up and, one by one, he placed a small quantity of the sauce in our mouths. We were all laughing, and hurting, and crying tears! Master was laughing, and his eyes were wet with loving tears of understanding. He laughed and laughed, and loved us so much. And we loved him, so much, for the precious moments of intimacy and gentle teasing.

Master then told us of an earlier episode in his life, when he had visited Mexico several years before. During meals a "contest" had unfolded, to see who among the participants could handle highly-spiced food. Master told us that he was served very hot food, time after time, and always passed the test because he had prepared himself ahead of time. Then, the other "contestants" prepared a trap. They stopped talking about the contest for several days, then one day served Master a meal lavishly laced with hot chili peppers. He laughed at the memory, and said, "They got me! I thought the top of my head was going to explode!"

Paramahansaji was an indefatigable worker. He pushed to get things done. He pushed his body. Those around him were driven to keep up with his pace. Sometimes he wouldn't eat or sleep, if there was a job that had to be completed. He excelled in fulfilling purposes! His unspoken motto was, "Why wait? Let's do it! God will take care of everything!" He worked. Those close to him worked. God did take care of everything.

He also knew his own destined life's work. He knew why he was born into the world; he knew ahead of time what his duty was; he even knew which disciples would, or would not, fulfill their purposes. Yet, he kept on keeping on. I never knew him to back away from any challenge. And I never knew him to back away from a decision when he knew it was right.

When Master was preparing his commentary on the *Bhagavad Gita*, he dictated the statement that Mahavatar Babaji was Krishna, and still in the same body because of his occasional experiencing of *kaya-kalpa* (a regeneration procedure known to yogis). Someone in the room said, "Oh, sir, we can't say that!" Master got up from his chair, paced around the room like a lion, and demanded, "Why can't we say that? It's true; Babaji is Krishna! I only speak the truth!"

After the dairy was sold I moved to the Phoenix Center. I scheduled my duties to afford ample time for study and meditation. Summers, I watered and maintained the lawns, cleaned and made repairs on the buildings, typed business letters, and prepared the chapel for Sunday services. Herbert was the minister, and I assisted him from time to time. Eventually, I was asked to conduct the Sunday evening discussions based on Master's lessons, and to teach an occasional hatha yoga class.

I established my own meditation routine, which worked well for me. I would wake at 3 A.M., bathe, and go into the chapel. Lighting the votive candles on the altar, I honored Christ, Divine Mother, and my guru line. After a long session of devotional chanting, I meditated. After an hour or so of meditation, when I felt the need to do so, I would again chant and pray until meditation began spontaneously. This continued until about 7 A.M.

After a light breakfast, I would begin my work day and continue until five, with a break at noon for an hour of meditation, followed by a lunch of fruit or vegetable salad. My evening meditation session would begin about 5:30 P.M. and continue until nine or ten o'clock.

There were many times when meditation did not come easily. At such times, I would pray more, chant longer, and sometimes just sit with eyes open, looking at the altar and letting thoughts flow as I observed them. Regardless of whether meditation was fruitful or not, I would sit for the agreed-upon period of time. This was my inner commitment to God and gurus. Almost two years were spent in this routine, with rare exceptions, such as when unexpected duties were pressing, or when I would go to visit Master in California.

I never suffered from hallucinations or experiences of "otherworldliness." I was calm, soul-centered and reflective. Living as a monk, I had no social life; I did not go to the theater, read magazines or listen to the radio. I did read the weekend edition of the newspaper.

I also read, many times, *Autobiography of a Yogi, The Bhagavad Gita,* selections from the *Holy Bible* and biographies of several Christian saints, among them St. Francis, St. Anthony, St. Theresa, and Brother Lawrence.

The following incident occurred during a visit with Master at his desert retreat. I was impatient at the time, because it seemed to me that my progress was slow. Master knew I had read, at his suggestion, about how St. Anthony had spent years in self-confined contemplation before experiencing illumination. He said to me on this occasion, "Think of St. Anthony, Roy, how patient he was!" I received his message but, at that time, St. Anthony's tribulations were the last thing I wanted to think about! No matter how impatient I might be, or how uncertain of my future good, only a few minutes with Paramahansaji sufficed to make me feel courageous and confident.

Only once did I disregard Master's advice, and he soon corrected me. The incident took place about six months after he had accepted me for discipleship. He had instructed me to read only his books, and a few others that he recommended, for the first year. The reason for this was twofold: first, what he initially asked me to read would take far more than a year of reading and rereading to fully appreciate and understand. He would sometimes say, "Read a little, think more, and meditate all the time." Secondly, he did not want new disciples to read too widely and as a result become confused.

There was also a deeper purpose. A disciple should never question the wisdom of his guru's instructions, because the guru knows better than the disciple what is important for the disciple. More important than reading, more important than anything a disciple might do, is for the disciple to maintain his attunement with the guru's consciousness and with his will. More than once I heard Master say, to me and to others, "If you will allow me, I will reveal God to you." Bear in mind that we are not here discussing a casual teacher-student relationship —we are examining the possibility of a newly-awakened soul being shown the way to liberation of consciousness!

It was only years later, after I had been teaching for a long time, that I fully comprehended the incredible responsibility

that falls upon a guru when he is working with disciples, and
how few are the truly dedicated disciples who come to a guru
for what the guru really has to offer them, if they are but able
to accept it.

One day, during the time while I was still at the goat dairy,
I was delivering milk to customers in nearby Scottsdale. I
noticed a bookstore in the heart of the village. I knew, as I
parked the truck and walked into the store, that I was in error,
because of Master's instructions to me. I knew, as I looked over
the titles displayed in the section reserved for books on Yoga,
that I was straying. Then a book titled *The Gospel of Sri
Ramakrishna* caught my eye. This huge volume was compiled
by Mahendranath Gupta, a disciple of the great master.

As I took the book from the shelf and began to examine it,
my mind rationalized, "Oh, this is all right, because Master
himself knew the author. When Master was a little boy he
used to visit the author, and even received a spiritual experience through his touch." In this way did I inwardly justify
my avid perusal and subsequent purchase of *The Gospel of Sri
Ramakrishna*!

I was so inwardly confident that my inner guidance was
correct that I found it expedient to conceal the fact of my purchase from Herbert and the other monks! I would read the
book during work breaks, going into my private room for the
purpose. The stories in the book were certainly fascinating!
Numerous accounts of visions, kundalini experiences, samadhi
experiences, and more. I noticed, however, that as the days
passed I was thinking more of Sri Ramakrishna, and of his experiences, than I was of my own guru line. My meditations
suffered also, because reading the book was consuming most
of my spare time.

Before long, it was time for my regular trip to California
to visit Master. This time, he was at Mt. Washington. I was
waiting with several of the monks when Master walked through
the lower hallway. Usually, when he hadn't seen me for a few
weeks, he would acknowledge me, give me a gentle hug and
tell me how happy he was that I had come to be with him. On
this occasion, things were different.

I noticed that Master saw me as soon as he entered the area. He knew I was supposed to be there and he glanced at me out of the corner of his eye, but he did not look directly at me or show any sign of recognition. No one else in that room knew what was taking place between us, but I knew exactly why he avoided me.

He walked slowly along the corridor, talking with one monk and then another. He pointedly walked right past me, not looking at me, so close that we brushed shoulders as he passed. Still, no acknowledgment. Pausing about two feet past me, he turned to one of the monks and said, "Roy is a spiritual prostitute!" Then silence. The others, of course, had no idea what he meant by the statement, and he did not explain it to them. He was speaking to another, but for my benefit, knowing that I would know exactly what he meant. He might have more accurately said, "Roy is a spiritual *adulterer*," because by reading material forbidden to me at that phase of my training I had, to a minor degree, mixed and diluted the spiritual influence in my own consciousness.

Master then turned to me, holding my gaze with his, and said, "I asked you to read only my books and a few others, for a purpose. After you are grounded in inner realization you can read anything without losing your attunement with me, or being confused. But for now, you should do as I say."

I said nothing. I folded my hands and knelt to touch his feet. When I stood up he smiled and touched me at the spiritual eye. He then murmured, "It's all right, it's all right." His tone was affectionate and forgiving, and the incident was over.

Master never had to lecture me. He had only to say a few words, when necessary, and I knew what he meant and what he expected of me. He knew it, too. He once said, to a group of disciples, "I love it when you do as I ask. I love it even more when I do not have to ask, when only a gesture or eye contact conveys the message."

During my intense meditation phase I learned much about myself, and I learned much about the validity of the yogic teachings. I had always read the four Gospels of the New Testament with reverence, but it was only as I experienced deeper meditation, and listened to Master discuss the teachings of Jesus, that the Christian scriptures came alive for me. I began to see clearly that one underlying truth supports all great religious traditions, and that the light shining through all avatars and prophets is God.

There is a vast difference between knowing *about* something and actually experiencing the reality of that which is being contemplated. For instance, it is one thing to intellectually acknowledge that the soul is a specialized unit of omnipresent Consciousness, and does not really need to identify with the mental field or the physical body in order to be real of itself, and it is quite another thing to comprehend this truth in one's own experience.

Once, in 1951, while meditating on a Sunday afternoon, I experienced myself as a unit of pure awareness. I had been calmly meditating for about an hour when suddenly, somewhere nearby, a door was slammed shut. I was indignant that anyone in the building would be so insensitive, because the rule was that quiet was to be observed in the building. After a moment or two, I returned full attention to the spiritual eye; instantly, I was no longer a person with a body, trying to meditate. I was a point of conscious awareness, with spherical vision, floating in a vast sea of blue space. It seemed that tiny sparkling white lights twinkled in the distance. The ocean of blue conscious light was still, yet vibrant with potential vitality. There was no sense of fear or strangeness, merely an awareness of being aware of the situation.

After a duration I returned to body identification. The inner awareness of the experience is vivid today. I have since experienced similar perceptions, during meditation and during occasions when awakening from sleep in the quiet of the night.

There were occasions, during that phase of my sadhana, when I would inwardly see saints and luminous personages whom I did not recognize. The influence was always benevolent, as though a stream of grace were flowing through them to me. I also experienced a degree of cosmic consciousness, during which I could perform my routine duties while, at the same time, I could be inwardly aware of myself as filling the universe.

There were also occasions of spontaneous energy flows through the chakras, and an extended period during which I experienced that the nervous system was being attuned and the brain ordered, as the mental field was being cleansed. I found that my powers of intuition became more pronounced, and that I could perceive the thoughts and intentions of others, as well as the inner meaning of the scriptures.

During this phase I also experimented with fasting, either drinking only water or subsisting on fresh grapes or fresh juices for a period. I was careful not to go to extremes, however, knowing that this could lead to impaired concentration and even to hallucinations during meditation.

During one summer I experienced powerful sexual desire, so much so that whenever I sat to meditate I would automatically envision beautiful women, and the various possibilities of sexual experience with them. While I knew this to be normal, I also experienced feelings of guilt, because I was a monk and had agreed to lead a celibate life. There is certainly nothing wrong or harmful about natural sexual urges, and it is not necessary that one be celibate in order to be successful on the spiritual path, but a monastic should not allow sexual urges, and their attendant fantasies, to intrude upon chosen purposes.

Later, when I visited Paramahansaji at Mt. Washington, he invited Herbert and me to visit him upstairs, near his apartment. He sat in a chair in the hall and talked with us about certain matters regarding the Phoenix Center. When church matters had been discussed, he said to Herbert, "You go on; I want to speak to Roy alone."

When he was certain that we were alone, he leaned in my direction and asked, "Are you having problems?"

His question, while not unexpected, caught me off guard and, before I could answer, he continued, "It's all right. It's normal for a young man to have such desires. But in your situation it disturbs your concentration. I'll tell you what to do."

He then advised me, as a father might a son, on certain

matters relating to directing sexual energies upwards to the heart center, and to the third eye, in order to transmute them.

Later, a brother disciple who had left the monastic life to marry, told me of how Master had counseled him, relating information from an ancient Indian manual dealing with romantic love.

Paramahansaji had early in life decided to be a monk, but he was not ignorant about male-female relationships. Because of this, he was able to advise both monastics and married couples in a very practical way.

I always visited Mt. Washington during the annual summer convocation, to which students from all over the country came to participate in classes and to receive Kriya Yoga initiation. It was after the initiation service in 1951 that Master named St. Lynn as his spiritual successor and conferred upon him the title of Rajarsi Janakananda. Janaka was an ancient Indian king who was also a saint. Mr. Lynn was a prosperous businessman who was also highly realized.

The monks and sisters were always invited to attend the annual Christmas banquet. Another banquet was held annually on the eve of Master's birthday, January 5th. It was during his last birthday celebration, in 1952, that he talked with us about his imminent passing. He said, "I will spend some time in space, and then be reborn in the Himalayas and be with Babaji."

He also said that evening, "I will one day return but you will not know me. My colors will be blue and gold."

Blue and gold were colors favored by Paramahansaji. Invariably he would have all of the chapels and church sanctuaries decorated with light blue walls and gold and white trim. Pale blue has a calming effect on the mind and is conducive to meditation.

In the fall of 1951, while I was at the Phoenix Center, we received a telephone call from Master. Herbert took the call and then passed the telephone to me for a moment. Sister Gyanamata had just made her transition and we were asked to attend her memorial service at the Hermitage in Encinitas.

Sister Gyanamata had been a devoted disciple for several years. She was an American, and Paramahansaji had given her the monastic name, which means "mother of wisdom." He once said of her, "She knows my every thought." He also said, "I will not long outlive Sister."

He later told us of how she had passed. She was elderly and had, several times, asked Master for permission to leave the body. He had always declined permission. He would tell her, "I need you for inspiration." He also wanted her to have the opportunity to experience full Self-realization before she departed.

He had been summoned to her room because she had become very weak. He sat with her and they talked. He asked her, "Do you have any desires? If you do, tell me right now and I will fulfill them at once." He did not want her to depart with any unfulfilled yearnings, nor with any regrets.

Hers had been a life of quiet devotion. She and St. Lynn would sometimes talk, and she knew of his dramatic, sometimes even cosmic, meditation experiences. She mentioned to Master that she sometimes felt that she had perhaps missed something because she had not usually experienced the more dramatic meditation perceptions.

Paramahansaji used to tell disciples a story, of a man who was invited to visit the king and went to the palace grounds. He was told to wait. While waiting, he wandered about the palace grounds and became so entranced with their beauty that he totally forgot his appointment with the king. The palace guards found him and escorted him to the gates. He was never asked to return.

Master used to say, "If he had kept his appointment with the king, and made friends with him, he could have had access to the palace grounds anytime." The moral was that if one would keep his appointment with God, and make friends with Him, one could have access to any part of the universe, subtle or gross, if one had such an inclination.

Sister Gyanamata knew this story, so when she mentioned that perhaps she might have missed something, Master told her, "Why do you want to wander about in the garden when you are already in the palace?" She understood and remained still.

After Master blessed her and left her room, he asked to be

driven to a spot overlooking the ocean. He told us, "As I sat there, suddenly a great wave of love filled my heart and then shot out over the ocean. I knew then that Sister had passed."

It was later reported that, after Master had left her room, she asked a sister disciple who was assigned to assist her, to help her to her meditation chair. Frail and weak as she was, she sat in her meditation seat and passed consciously from the body.

The ability to assist disciples to make their transition from this world to the subtle realms was known to Paramahansaji. On several occasions, over the years, he would tell close disciples, "So and so recently passed. I was there and helped him into the next world."

He was once writing at Encinitas when he asked his secretaries to leave the room. Later, he summoned them and told them that he had "just been" to San Diego, some twenty-five miles distant, to assist the wife of a close disciple as she made her transition. Those who had been in the hospital room confirmed Master's explanation of what had happened.

The woman was friendly to Master during her lifetime but sometimes indicated resentment because her husband was so involved with the work. Shortly before her transition she had been hospitalized because cancer had ravaged her body. She experienced considerable pain and drugs were no longer adequate to allow her to be comfortable. Master had visited her at the hospital. When he emerged from her room he said to her husband, "I cannot heal her, but I have taken away the pain."

When she did pass, those in the room felt Paramahansaji's presence, and she said before she passed, "Yogananda is here."

Even a great master cannot always intrude upon a person's personal wishes or karmic condition. Usually, there must be an agreement on the part of the one needing healing, before a master can assume the responsibility of setting the healing forces in action.

During my early weeks at Mt. Washington, before being sent to Arizona, an incident relating to healing transpired. An older man had been living on the property. He was a carpenter, and helped to maintain various properties. He once said to a

group of younger monks, "I wish I had your faith. I have
studied so many things over the years before coming here. I
believe in Master and I trust him, but I just don't have the faith
I should have."

He became ill and was taken to a hospital. One evening,
late, Master returned to Mt. Washington, and as his car stopped
at the lower entrance, a few monks happened to be there. He
opened the car door and talked with us for a while.

"I have just come from seeing Mr. Brockway," he said. "It
was so sad. I said to him, 'Mr. Brockway, do you want me to
heal you? If you do, tell me, and I will heal you right now.' He
was so weak. He said, 'No, sir.'"

Master paused, then said, "If he had said 'yes' I could have
healed him."

A master sometimes intercedes, even when a disciple does
not ask for help, because the disciple has given prior permission
or is open to the assistance. But even an unawakened person
has free will, and the freedom to determine his own happiness
or unhappiness. A master can point the way, and provide whatever help the disciple is willing to accept, but it is up to the
disciple to be willing to experience transformation and needed
change.

I always found that when I was in tune with my guru my
meditations were deeper, I was more calm and peaceful, and
circumstances in my life unfolded in more orderly fashion. A
true guru does not stand between God and the disciple. A true
guru is a conduit through which divine energies can flow to the
disciple who is responsive to them.

Paramahansaji would sometimes say, "I am not the guru.
God is the guru. I am but His servant." He played the role of
guru, but he was only fulfilling the will of God.

It was at the desert retreat that I last saw my guru in the
flesh. I had been invited to visit him just a few weeks prior to
his *mahasamadhi*, a yogi's conscious exit from the body. We
were sitting in the living room of his house. One of his secretaries brought him a glass of fruit juice and waited until she
was sure he drank it.

When she had left the room Master said, "See, for years I

Lahiri Mahasaya, guru of Swami Sri Yukteswar.

never paid much attention to regular eating. Now, they make me do it." Then he said, "Take care of your body, Roy; you have much work to do and you must be healthy." We talked for a while. He was smiling and vital. He said, "I just finished the *Gita*. Now my work is done. A little while ago, after I had completed the final chapter, I was sitting here, meditating. I saw a gold circle of light at the spiritual eye. I opened my eyes and saw the gold circle of light, there on the wall. Then I saw Babaji, Lahiri, and Sri Yukteswar appear in the light, in succession. They had come to thank me for finishing the work on the *Gita*."

Then he looked into my eyes. We were sitting very close. He said, "Roy, don't bother yourself with whether or not others seem intent on the path, whether they talk too much or waste their time. The important thing is that you go all the way in this lifetime. And you can do it. You must do it. Sri Yukteswar used to say, 'The boat that carries souls across the river of delusion to the far shore of Self-realization is ready to depart. Who will go? Who will go? If no one goes, I will go!' You must be like that!"

He paused, as though reflecting upon something, then continued, "Before Sri Yukteswar passed, we were sitting together and he suddenly trembled. I asked him what was the matter. He said, 'Just as a caged bird is sometimes reluctant to leave its cage, in exchange for freedom, so sometimes the soul is reluctant to leave the cage of the body in order to experience omnipresence.' He had been thinking of his departure soon to come." Master gazed more intently into my eyes. "Do you understand?" he asked. I knew what he meant, and that he was preparing for the near future event of his own departure.

Paramahansaji was very open with disciples in whom he had confidence. When we would walk the grounds of the desert retreat he would invite my questions and, always, answered them completely.

During my first year with him I asked, "Sir, have I been with you before?" He responded, "How could you be with me now if you had not been with me before? Of course, you have been with me before, and you will be with me many times in

Mahavatar Babaji, guru of Lahiri Mahasaya.

the future. You have come, as have some others, to help me with this work."

On that same occasion I asked a question which, in retrospect, seems a bit adventuresome, but he hesitated not a moment when answering it. I asked, "Sir, how many of the masters mentioned in your book (*Autobiography of a Yogi*) are fully liberated?"

He smiled and replied, "Not many. Many saints are content to roam in God for years, because it is so blissful. Only a few have the desire to go all the way."

This side of the transcendental field the possibilities for experience, in the myriad astral and causal realms, are almost limitless. Beyond these realms, even beyond the realm of the Godhead, is the undisturbed field of Pure Being. The yogi should have as his intention the conscious experience of this field of Pure Being, because this side of the field one is somewhat subject to the influence of nature's forces and inclinations.

Whenever I visited Mt. Washington I always participated in the morning and evening meditations. During the days, because my visits were always of a few days' duration, I rested, meditated, read, and discussed administrative details concerning the Phoenix Center with the treasurer and other officers of the board of directors. Sometimes Master would call me to his room to talk, or we would meet on the grounds.

An older minister once said to him, "Sir, isn't Roy too new with us to be so far away in Phoenix?" He felt that it was unusual for me to have been sent there without having spent many months, or years, at headquarters.

Master replied, "You leave my boy alone. I know what I'm doing."

During my years with him he did not give monastic names to resident disciples, with rare exceptions. Nor would he allow the men to wear beards or long hair. Swami Kriyananda (Donald Walters) was an exception where a beard was concerned. Master told him to grow a beard. "It will make you look older," he counseled.

The male disciples wore ordinary casual clothes when

working on the grounds. They were advised to dress neatly and to keep their hair trimmed. Good grooming was important, Master told us, "because people will watch you." Ministers could wear a white robe when conducting church services or counseling students. He told Herbert and me to wear robes when counseling people, adding this practical explanation: "You are young, and they will have more respect for what you say if you dress like a minister." He once advised me to be sure to keep my shoes polished, even the backs of them, "because people will look at you when you walk away, and you want everything to be just right. Don't do anything to cause others to find fault with you."

I never saw Master when he was not perfectly groomed. He was always clean and wore fresh clothing. His purity, with its origins at the soul level, extended to his dress, his manner, and his speech.

He was always courteous. We might have a late night conversation of an intimate nature, yet the next day he would greet me with, "How are you, Roy?" and his inquiry would be warm and honest. Even with disciples of long standing, he was always polite when he talked with them.

He would counsel us, "Be cheerful but grave," meaning "Be pleasant, but remain centered." He might tell humorous stories (which he often did) until the listeners, and he himself, were reduced to almost uncontrollable laughter. Then, in a moment, he would turn a phrase and discuss matters of philosophical import, and the mood was again returned to one of courteous rapport.

It was late in the evening of March 7, 1952 that Herbert telephoned from Los Angeles. He was quiet and said, "Master passed tonight. Conduct a memorial service there for the members and then come here right afterward. I'll give you more details when I see you."

I contacted as many center members as I could and asked them to pass the word to others whom they knew. At the simple memorial service, I spoke but a few words, led a meditation, and invited the members to come forward to place a flower before a photograph of Paramahansaji. It was a quiet service and love was there.

On my arrival at Mt. Washington, I was immediately taken to Master's apartment. His body lay on the bed, dressed in his ochre robe. Brother and sister disciples came and went in silence, except for an occasional controlled evidence of grief.

I cannot fully explain to the average reader's satisfaction my feelings of that moment. I had grown up with an inner awareness of the presence of God in my life. I had been very close to departing from this world when I was eighteen, during a protracted illness. I had experienced my mother's sudden transition. I had meditated deeply for two years as a disciple of my guru. I had learned to be attuned to him and the guru line during our occasions of physical separation. In mind and consciousness I had roamed the universe and communed with the saints. Now, I stood at Master's side and knew he would not open his eyes and smile that sweet smile of recognition. There was an inner understanding. There was that moment of knowing. There was no feeling of desolation or lack, but there was a feeling of loss. I had loved him so, and I loved him still. Now, however, I could only commune with him inwardly. I would no longer feel the touch of his hand in blessing, no longer touch him with tender care when he would invite a helping hand to assist him into his car, or up a stair, or when he would reach out to invite closeness as we walked together.

There would be no physical contact now, but there would be no real sense of loss. There are memories, and there are occasions of inner plane communion, when the heart is made glad and the soul enriched. Victory to the true guru, who is the embodiment of God for each of us!

Hundreds of disciples and friends gathered at Mt. Washington for the final memorial service. Master's body, in a bronze casket, was in front, just before the altar. During the service, Dr. Lewis read appropriate selections from *The Holy Bible* and *The Bhagavad Gita.* Swami Premananda, then minister of the SRF church in Washington, D.C., performed vedic rites to symbolically release the soul from all earthly ties. Rajarsi spoke a few quiet words, and seemed to me to be sad, even

Paramahansa Yogananda blessing Rajarsi Janakananda and naming him as his spiritual successor, 1951.

though a divine flow emanated from him. India's ambassador to the United States, Binay R. Sen, delivered a moving address, during which he mentioned that while he and his party were being driven to the top of Mt. Washington earlier, they had seen a rainbow in the sky, an auspicious occurrence.

I still remember the love in that room that day. To conclude the service, everyone slowly walked by to view Master's countenance for the final time, and we dropped rose petals on the casket, all the while softly chanting, as a group, "Aum guru, aum guru, aum guru, aum guru."

The body was then taken to Forest Lawn Memorial Park, there later to be placed in a crypt. I sought out a secluded place behind the main building, where I could be alone, and wept. When I had become somewhat composed, I walked about the grounds, hoping to be alone with my thoughts. I encountered Oliver Black, and he shared private words of comfort and understanding. He told me that when, a few days before, he had conducted a memorial service in Detroit for SRF students there, Master's presence was felt by everyone.

Paramahansaji had celebrated his fifty-ninth birthday two months prior to his *mahasamadhi*, a yogi's conscious exit from the body. Because he was a spiritual master, he knew his past and his future, and he knew what his mission on earth was to be. He was to lay the foundation for yoga in the West, work with disciples who would be led to him, and write his many books.

The days before his departure were active ones. He had returned to Mt. Washington from his desert retreat on March 4, 1952, to greet Ambassador Sen and his party. He hosted them at Mt. Washington and presented them with token gifts. On another day, Master asked to be driven to the Lake Shrine in Pacific Palisades. There he walked the grounds, sat at the chapel organ, playing and chanting for a long time, then had lunch with a few disciples. Upon returning to Mt. Washington that day, he asked to be driven to a vantage point where he could look at the buildings and property, giving some advice on repairs and improvements to those who were with him.

Herbert Freed was with Master that day and was told of

future unfoldments of the work. During one discussion Master said, "I have an opportunity to start another work in the mid-west, very similar to this one, but one that would not interfere with this one at all."

On March 7th, Master remained in his room, for the most part sitting in meditative silence. Later in the day he was driven to the Biltmore Hotel in downtown Los Angeles and was checked into a suite. "Imagine," he said, "I have a room at the Biltmore!" He was remembering his first visit to Los Angeles in 1925, when he had stayed at the Biltmore Hotel and lectured to overflow audiences in a nearby auditorium. Thousands were turned away because the huge facility could not accommodate the crowd.

A banquet in honor of Ambassador Sen was scheduled that evening, and Master had been invited to be one of the guest speakers. During the event those who could observe him noticed that he was very quiet, though attentive to others. When he was introduced to speak, as he stood up he said to Mrs. Sharma, a guest, "Always remember: life has its beautiful roses, and it has its thorns; and we must accept both."

He spoke quietly for a few minutes, telling of some of his early experiences in America, and calling for cooperation among the peoples of the earth to ensure a world of peace and harmony. He concluded by reciting a poem he had composed years before, "My Mother India." As he completed the final line, "I am hallowed, my body touched that sacred sod," he turned to his right and slipped free of the body.

Weeks later, news media carried a story telling of a report made by the directors of Forest Lawn, revealing that for over four weeks after Paramahansaji had left his body, the body had shown no visible evidence of disintegration. The casket had not been sealed, because representatives of Yogoda Satsanga, the Indian branch of Master's work, were expected to visit the United States to view the body. Finally, the lid was put in place and sealed, and Master's body was placed in a crypt. Fresh flowers are always before it and it remains a pilgrimage site today. From time to time, when I visit Los Angeles, I drive to Forest Lawn to spend a few quiet minutes there.

FOUR

Ordination into
an Ancient Tradition

While still at Mount Washington, I was presented with a certificate of ordination. Because Master had passed two days before my twenty-first birthday, the age when I could legally be recognized as an ordained minister in the state of California, the certificate carries the signature of Rajarsi Janakananda (St. Lynn's monastic name) and that of the secretary of the Self-Realization Fellowship, Florina Darling. A copy of that certificate now hangs on my office wall at CSA in Lakemont, Georgia.

Paramahansaji had actually ordained me much earlier, in the late autumn of the preceding year. Herbert Freed and I were then visiting Mt. Washington for a few days, and Master asked us to meet him in the hallway near his apartment on the upper floor of the main building. After giving us some advice about the Phoenix Center, he turned to me and said, "Kneel down." I knelt by his chair and he placed his hands on my head.

He spoke with quiet authority and intention. "I ordain you a minister of Self-Realization, and I empower you to represent God and the line of gurus. Teach others as I have taught, heal others as I have healed, and initiate them into the science of Kriya Yoga."

Herbert was visibly surprised, and he asked Master, "Sir, do you mean that we are to initiate people into Kriya Yoga?" He asked this question because he knew, as did I, that only Master and a few selected ministers at the time conducted Kriya Yoga initiation services.

Master looked at him and exclaimed, "Why not? The same God is in you that is in me! What I have done, you should do!"

I did not actually initiate others into Kriya Yoga until some years later, after I had left the organization. I did, however, with Master's permission, instruct students in the practice of mantra and the technique of listening to the inner sound and concentrating upon the light of the spiritual eye. I also reviewed the kriya process with those who had already been initiated by Master or one of the senior ministers.

During that few minutes in the hallway with Master, I became a teaching representative of a tradition which has its roots in the distant past; some say it goes back one hundred thousand years, others that the tradition existed in subtle realms before the worlds were formed.

A minister in this tradition is one through whom God's reality can be shared with seeking souls. This cannot be guaranteed by having a ministerial candidate successfully complete a few years of study; it can be valid only when the person called to the ministry is sufficiently devoid of ego, and open to God's will, so that grace can flow.

Through Paramahansaji and my guru line I am spiritually and telepathically connected with a line of enlightened masters whose influence extends into the present. A representative of this tradition does not simply teach what his predecessors taught. A representative of this tradition is the embodiment of the teaching. Through him or her are transmitted the consciousness and spiritual energies of God.

There are many ministers today who have been licensed to teach by a recognized school, but whose lives have not yet been transformed by the infilling of the spirit of God. Their efforts, then, are fruitless. They may teach the principles, they may guide the needy, they may do much good at the level of human consciousness, but the power of God is not evident.

It was Master's way to carefully observe his disciples, to note the unfoldment of their inner capacities. When he felt a disciple was ready to represent him, and the tradition of which he was a guru, he would ordain that disciple. Some were surprised when he ordained them, and would even express their feelings about how they did not feel adequate to the responsibility. Master would say, "God tells me who is ready and who is not. I do not make mistakes."

On one occasion when I was talking to him, he looked at me and said, "You died young last time. You would have died young this time, too, but your love for God pulled you through." He was referring to the months before we met, when I was ill.

As I was leaving Mount Washington after Master's funeral service, Faye Wright (later to become the third president of Self-Realization Fellowship and to be known as Sister Dayamata) informed me that it was Master's wish, as expressed to her earlier by him, that I become the minister of the Phoenix center and that Herbert remain in California and be assigned other duties.

My routine in Phoenix remained as before, with the addition of preparing and delivering the Sunday morning and midweek classes. The congregation remained small in numbers, but the majority were devoted to the work and proved loyal and supportive. One of the stalwart members at the time was Mrs. Anna Coates. She attended every service, and whenever any volunteer work was needed, she was always the first to respond. It was a joy, three decades after I had left the monastic order, to attend services at the Self-Realization Temple in Phoenix and to be greeted by Anna who, nearing age ninety, was still greeting devotees as they entered the sanctuary. She and others like her represent the best in devotion to God's work.

Master loved the Phoenix center. He dedicated the facility in 1949, and always talked to me and to Herbert about the future of the work in Arizona. Over and over he reminded us, "God is the honey, the church is the hive. Make sure that God's presence is there. That alone will feed the people."

The first Phoenix center, where I served, was located at the corner of Eighteenth Street and West Monroe, less than two hundred yards from the State Capitol complex. Different buildings now occupy that space and a new temple was dedicated several years ago by Sister Dayamata. The current facility is an architectural wonder located on North Central Avenue in Phoenix; I go there to meditate and attend services whenever I am in that city.

Even though Paramahansaji was no longer with us in the body, my inner attunement with him remained undiminished. He was in my mind and heart every moment of each day, as he is now. Especially during occasions of quiet contemplation, after meditation, I would feel his presence, and his strength and love. Now, as then, when I feel his presence there is also the vivid awareness of the presence and influence of Sri Yukteswar, Lahiri and Babaji. It is then that I know that I am truly anchored in a teaching tradition through which God's influence is extended into the world.

During the first year as minister in Phoenix I learned much. It was often Master's way to put a person into a situation where he knew the person could excel, and then leave that person to learn for himself how to do things. Those who possess the inner capacities to succeed will do so; those who do not will learn some valuable lessons.

I seldom needed to go far from the center to take care of matters related to the ministry. When I did travel on errands, I used the city bus or a bicycle. Later an automobile of antique vintage was donated to the center. With the help of some of the members, the interior of the building was painted and a new altar installed in the chapel. I was careful to see that the building and grounds were maintained in perfect condition, because this was Master's wish. Many who read this book, and who have visited any of the churches and centers maintained by his organization, will agree that they are always beautifully designed and maintained. Master's ideal was that a church, shrine or retreat facility should reflect purity and order, and should offer devotees and visitors the most supportive environment for quiet reflection and soul upliftment.

From my boyhood I have felt love for Jesus, an avatar of God. It was Master who taught me to understand Jesus' ministry and to love him more. When I was with my guru he advised me to read several biographical accounts of Catholic saints. A wooden crucifix adorned the wall of my room, along with pictures of Jesus and my guru line. Master once casually mentioned to a disciple that he remembered a previous embodiment when he had played the role of a known Catholic saint. He was always respectful of that tradition; indeed, he was respectful of all traditions based on devotion and duty to God's will.

Paramahansaji was universal in his understanding and often spoke of how useful it would be for the people of the world to learn to exemplify the best of Eastern spirituality and Western practicality. He was himself an example of this ideal, and he frequently praised many of his American disciples for their actualization of this ideal.

As before, I visited the California Self-Realization centers on a regular schedule, to discuss organizational matters and to see St. Lynn, when he was available. After Master passed, St. Lynn increasingly radiated Master's consciousness, and to be able to sit quietly with him and meditate was always a profound experience.

As a young man of sixteen years of age, St. Lynn had traveled from his home in Louisiana to Kansas City, Missouri. There he supported himself and attended night school, studying law and accounting. As an accountant for an insurance firm he excelled, and when the president retired, James J. Lynn purchased the company. Over the years, his business skills resulted in his becoming a recognized influence in the financial circles of Kansas City. Eventually he was to become president of several insurance companies, to sit on the boards of banks and railroads, and to own a company which was heavily involved in the oil business.

St. Lynn met Paramahansaji when he was in his thirties. Already a millionaire, he still lacked inner peace. One evening he attended a public lecture and sat in the back of the auditorium. He told us that he saw a light come from Master's body and flow across the room to where he sat, and he was flooded with inner calm and peace. Later, when Master initiated him into the practice of Kriya Yoga meditation, they sat together in meditation and St. Lynn experienced an ecstatic state. Years later, as a result of his deep meditation practice, he experienced the highest states of God-communion.

Master told us that St. Lynn had been a yogi in the previous incarnation and had returned this time to help him with the work and to experience liberation of consciousness. Over the years St. Lynn contributed several million dollars to the work; in his final years, he retired to a farm in southern California to devote himself to deeper meditation. He told of a few of his inner perceptions from time to time.

Once, when he began to meditate early in the morning, he was not able to perceive the inner light. The awareness of the presence of God was absent. Focusing his attention at the spiritual eye with persistence, he was able to perceive a pinpoint of light. Then, he became that light and, gradually, as conscious light he felt himself expanding until, as conscious light, his awareness was extended throughout his body, then beyond it, to fill the universe. He experienced himself as conscious light, and as being the universe and all manifestations of it. When he emerged from that experience he found that over six hours had passed; he never again was devoid of the inner awareness of his true nature.

On another, earlier occasion he experienced difficulty in practicing certain advanced meditation procedures. As he meditated, he was visited by Babaji, on the inner planes, and shown how to rise above body consciousness and practice meditation in his subtle form.

Few of St. Lynn's business associates knew of his involvement in yoga. He told me once that one of his close associates used to tease him and suggest that if he continued to be so involved with yoga he would lose his "business touch." He chuckled at the memory and said, "Business has never been better!"

Even though he was generous, like many who have worked hard to become highly successful, he was very careful about expenditures. Master once told me of how he had confronted St. Lynn about his occasional reluctance to give freely. The occasion was just a year or so before Master's passing. He and St. Lynn were sitting together, and Master felt it was the moment to address the matter. His function, as guru, was to clear away anything in his disciple's consciousness which might prevent his final enlightenment.

"St. Lynn is a beautiful example of this work," Master told me, "but there was this one thing in his mind that could have held him back and I knew I had to do something about it. In all of the years we have been together we have never discussed business. We have only talked of God and communed with Him. We needed that piece of property overlooking the Lake Shrine, so we could keep it from being developed and have it ruin the seclusion of the place. I was given the first opportunity to buy it and the price was thirty thousand dollars. I told St. Lynn of the need and then I looked at him and asked, 'Will you buy it for me?' I had never asked him for money before and it caught him by surprise. For the first time in our relationship he would not look at me. Finally, he did look at me and tears were running down his cheeks, and he said, 'Yes, sir.' That was the last little thing that he had to face and get out of his consciousness, that little attachment to money."

Another brother disciple whom I always enjoyed being with was J. Oliver Black. Oliver also met Master when he himself was in business in Detroit, and Master was visiting that city. Oliver has said that he was teaching yoga before he even knew what yoga was! Master told him of his past incarnations and spent ten days with him, teaching him the basics of Kriya Yoga and of many healing methods. Oliver later became a minister and for years conducted Sunday services and midweek classes. He was also given permission to conduct Kriya initiation services.

Years later, after Master had gone into relative seclusion at the desert retreat, he once called Oliver in Detroit and asked him to initiate two men who were visiting from Mexico. He assured Oliver that he would be "with him" during the initia-

Paramahansa Yogananda, hands upraised in blessing.

tion service. The men arrived and a time was set for their initiation. It took place in Oliver's office.

"After the initiation, we were meditating," Oliver said. "Suddenly, I heard a sound, like a strong breeze blowing. I opened my eyes but didn't see anything. After a while I heard the sound again. Opening my eyes, I saw Master standing there. One of the men began to cry and the other one felt "electricity" go through his body. When I got home that night the telephone was ringing. I answered it and it was Master. The first thing he said was, "See, Oliver, I told you I'd be with you!"

After his retirement from business responsibilities, Oliver founded Song of the Morning Ranch in northern Michigan, a yoga center set amidst the beauty of over 800 acres of wooded land. In 1985, the Golden Lotus Colony, a spiritual community, was planned and development started.

Whenever I would visit SRF headquarters, during summer convocations, a highlight was always the opportunity for several of the monks to gather around Oliver and ask him to share stories about Master. He was always extremely supportive and generous with his time, and the spiritual joy that bubbled to the surface and spread from him to all in the group was an inspiration.

During the early months of 1953, I began to feel that I should withdraw from monastic life. My love for God and my devotion to the work remained undiminished, but it seemed to me necessary to learn to relate to a larger world. I was at home with the interior life but my understanding of the outer life was incomplete. I was then twenty-two years of age and had spent my first eighteen years in a rural community and then over three years as a monastic.

After much soul-searching I contacted Sister Dayamata and asked to see her. We met a few days later and talked openly about many things. She confided to me some of her earlier challenges on the path and gave me wise counsel. One of the matters we discussed was that of my representing SRF as a minister. At that time, with few exceptions which Master had made, the policy was that ministers be monastics. It was

discussed that perhaps, if I left the order, I could still be a
teacher and direct another center activity, but that would have
to wait until I had become settled in another city, away from
Phoenix. We agreed that it would not be appropriate for me to
continue as a teacher in the city where I was known to have
been active as a minister. The important matter was that the
center in Phoenix remain strong and that members not be challenged by organizational change.

Sister Dayamata asked me if I felt that a change of duties,
perhaps moving from Phoenix to one of the other SRF centers,
would be helpful to me. I explained to her that I did not think
so. I was content with my duties at the Phoenix center and I
was inwardly dedicated to God and my guru's teaching tradition. My inner guidance was that I needed experience outside
of the monastic environment, to learn and to grow. It was
agreed that I would remain as minister of the Phoenix center
until I had made my final decision, and that the matter would
not be discussed with anyone other than members of the
executive board of the organization.

I was not asked to leave; I had done nothing to misrepre-
sent Master's teaching, and my relationships with my brothers and sisters of the order remained warm and cordial. When
I finally decided to depart, in autumn of that year, it was with
a heavy heart, yet with a sense of inner guidance that the
move was appropriate.

I do not know what the general attitude is today about
those who leave the SRF monastic environment. When I was
still there the attitude of many in the organization was pro-
vincial: if one left one was considered to have gotten off the
path, and perhaps it would take several incarnations to be
drawn back to it. It was as though being "inside" was proof
of rightness and being "outside" was evidence of "sometimes
all right but not as good." Too many temptations existed in
the world; if one left the order it was an indication of lack of
inner strength, and obviously one had failed a spiritual test.
The result was that many who remained felt somewhat smug
in their secure situation, while many who left, even if their

lives were exemplary and their inner attunement with God undefiled, felt for a time a sense of guilt about their actions.

I am pleased to be able to say that over the years my personal relationship with Sister Dayamata and a few other brother and sister disciples has remained as loving and caring as it was when I was a member of the monastic order. I have been informed by others that a few brother disciples, those who never really knew me when I was there, because I spent most of my time at the Phoenix center and seldom participated in group activities at the California centers, have said various untrue and unkind things, such as: My subsequent work and ministry is the result of ego; I am deluded and am incurring much bad karma because of my actions; I am using Master's name to build my own reputation, and so on.

A frequent statement, which is reported to me by friends and disciples to whom I have suggested a visit to SRF centers, is that I am not "authorized" to initiate into kriya yoga. The unfortunate thing about that statement is that it confuses the devotee to whom it is addressed. If I am not authorized to initiate people into kriya yoga, why do they feel such love for God and experience such positive benefits from their spiritual practices as a result of having studied with me? Mainly, the reaction of the students is, why does there have to be this contention among those who are supposed to be united in working for a better world?

To set the record straight, and to make the matter clear, I was ordained by Master and authorized by him to teach and to represent the kriya yoga tradition. This was acknowledged by the executive board of the organization. I am not authorized by the organization because I am not a part of it; I am authorized because I am a disciple of my guru, who directly charged me with the responsibility.

Another matter which has confused many people is that of an announcement which has been published stating that Paramahansa Yogananda was the last in the line of SRF gurus and that, henceforth, his teachings will be the guru for the members of the movement. Notice the wording here, that he is the *last of the line of SRF gurus.* What the statement reveals is that the organization will not recognize any other person as guru *of that organization.* It is impossible for any person, or group, to declare that the guru-disciple tradition and transmission can end. Wherever there is a disciple of a true guru who has received through the guru the grace to allow God's goodness to flow, the guru-disciple line will continue. It is not something that can be decided upon by human invention or decision, any more than the validity of reincarnation was changed by a group of Church representatives in the third century. Human opinion and behavior is one thing; what is true is another.

The years which followed my departure from SRF have been ones which have allowed me the opportunity to more clearly understand the teachings of the masters, and to enter into a conscious relationship with the Larger Life.

Hundreds of thousands of people have been turned more Godward as a result of this ministry. Among them are many who would not have otherwise experienced that connection.

FIVE

Years of Change, Years of Grace

For a few months after I resigned from the organization, I did little; most of my waking hours were spent in self-examination and waiting, waiting for guidance. It was an interesting time in my life, knowing of the inner call to minister, yet without any clear sense of direction. Then, early in 1954, I received in the mail a letter "inviting" me to enlist in the U.S. Army. As an active minister I had been exempt from the draft, but now I was available.

I volunteered to serve two years in the medical corps. After basic training, which was a maturing experience, I was sent to Fort Sam Houston, in San Antonio, Texas, for advanced training. There, one evening while I was engaged in mopping the floor of the mess hall, I heard a familiar voice call to me, "Roy, Roy!" Turning toward the entrance door, I was surprised and pleased to see a brother disciple, Bill Brown. He was in the unit next to mine and had somehow learned I was there. After this Bill and I spent many off-duty hours together. A most joyous reunion! Bill had been at Mount Washington from his early teenage years, along with his mother and two sisters. His younger sister, Mrinalini Mata, was later to become a member of the Board of Directors of SRF.

Greeting a workshop group prior to program, Northern California, 1975.

Bill was then driving a pale green Plymouth of about 1939 vintage. One day he told me that his next duty tour was to be somewhere in Europe, and he offered me the car for one dollar. During the following six weeks, while I lived in Temple, Texas, I used the vehicle every other week to carpool fellow army friends to Fort Hood some forty miles distant, where I had been given temporary duty. They dubbed it the "green camel," because it never failed to get us to and from the base.

At Fort Hood I served in various hospital sections, learning basic procedures. While working in surgery I was amazed to observe the professional skill of the doctors and nurses. Indeed, during the following months, first at Fort Knox, Kentucky, then at Fort Riley, Kansas, it was a valuable learning experience for me to work closely with the professional staffs and to observe that patient care was so very important. At Fort Knox I worked in the clinic which handled morning out-patient demands, as well as afternoon sessions of blood-typing and routine processing of new recruits. At Fort Riley I was assigned to the upper respiratory ward, where the majority of patients were sent to recover from the common cold, flu, or just plain tiredness. An enema, plenty of bed rest, sometimes injections of antibiotics, and patients were soon back to their duty stations.

While in the army I made it a point to meditate regularly, often going to the base chapel, which was seldom used except for the occasions of announced services. Most of my friends called me "Rev," because they knew I was a minister. A few, knowing of my background, became close friends and confided their own interest in yoga and matters relating to a closer walk with God. It was a joy, many years later during a lecture visit to Chicago, Illinois, to again meet Stu Olsen, with whom I had shared many hours of friendship and deep discussion during my months at Fort Riley.

One morning, shortly after I had gone on duty, a friend came in from the adjoining hospital ward and handed me a copy of that day's edition of the *Kansas City Star*. Dominating the front page was a feature story telling of the passing of St. Lynn. Born in a one-room log cabin near Archibald, Louisiana,

Entrance to CSA, Lakemont.

in 1892, St. Lynn had moved into the field of God while in the bedroom of his spacious home in Borrego Springs, California, on February 20, 1955.

While on a three-day leave, I visited Unity School of Practical Christianity, a few miles outside of Kansas City, Missouri. There I met Lowell Fillmore, one of the sons of co-founder Charles Fillmore, Richard Lynch, and others. I was given a tour of the grounds and buildings, and marveled at the printing presses turning out hundreds of thousands of Unity magazines and pamphlets. A few years later, I was to be a frequent speaker at many Unity churches and centers, and I would even speak during a Sunday morning service at the Unity School.

Charles and Myrtle Fillmore founded Unity in the latter part of the last century. Charles Fillmore would at times confide to friends that he felt himself to be a reincarnated yogi and, indeed, his emphasis upon vegetarianism, deep meditation, and the regeneration of the body is very much a part of yogic tradition. Millions of people today read the inspirational magazine, *The Daily Word*, which has been published by Unity for decades.

As the days until my discharge from the army became fewer, I began to anticipate a return to ministering as a lay teacher for SRF. I decided upon Denver, Colorado, as the city in which to live, and thought for a time of attending chiropractic school in order to have a profession which would be of service and afford me an income. When I wrote to the board of directors of SRF about my plans, however, after a long delay I was informed by them that they no longer wanted me to represent them.

What to do? I prayed about the matter, then decided that since I was called to the ministry I would simply have to minister without organizational affiliation or support. Upon being discharged in March of 1956, I settled in Denver, renting two apartments which were part of a row of such dwellings. I used one apartment for living quarters; in the other, using the money received when discharged, I decorated a chapel and book room. Then, placing advertisements in the local newspapers, I announced a public lecture at a downtown location. Seventy people responded to the announcement and a small study group was organized. I offered Sunday morning services and midweek classes. Attendance was modest but those who did attend were dedicated. Financial support, however, was not generous enough to meet the needs of the ministry.

A move was made to another location, a two-story house with an apartment upstairs and a large room downstairs which was to serve as the chapel. I named the ministry The Shrine of All Faiths, and envisioned a large retreat facility in the Rocky Mountains. I had the dream, but I did not, at that time, have the consciousness to see the dream embodied.

I began to write articles for small-circulation publications with readerships made up of persons interested in metaphysical matters. I also wrote and published a booklet, *The Art of Living.* Fired with enthusiasm about the envisioned retreat facility, I wrote letters to people whom I thought would be interested in financially supporting such a project. In every instance except one I received by return mail a polite, "We wish you well but we can't be of practical assistance" response. The one person who wrote at length and offered sound advice was Father Divine. Although I do not have his original letters to me, I can quote them from memory.

"If your plan is of God," he wrote, "then it will be fulfilled. I would recommend that you take a job, and from your savings, begin." Again, "I do not believe in taking from people in order to give something back to them. Jesus said, 'Feed my sheep'; he didn't say, 'fleece my sheep.'"

It was not until some time later that I realized the scope of his work, and I have ever since been deeply touched that he would take the time and concern to write to me so clearly and at length.

I had first heard of Father Divine when I was about fifteen years of age, when newspapers carried stories about him from time to time. When I read about him, something in me felt a sense of certainty about him, and even though many of the newspaper articles were biased against him, I intuitively felt that he was a good person. My intuition was confirmed years later, when I met him. Of this, more later.

During my first year in Denver, several SRF members, men and women who were taking lessons by mail, attended my classes. There were also, among those who attended, members of various New Thought churches in the area. Twice, swamis visiting from India asked to be sponsored, and I was happy to do it even though in both instances I was to learn that they were more interested in attracting converts to their own cause than in supporting my work.

We can never know through whom our good will flow. One woman who used to attend the Denver programs had recently moved there from the midwest. Although she usually dramatized a gloomy attitude, she was a kind and gentle person. One day she handed me a small booklet by Joel S. Goldsmith. I had not until then heard of Mr. Goldsmith, but as I read the booklet I felt very good about what he had to share. Two days later the woman called me and said, "I've arranged for you to see Joel tomorrow. He's in town to see his students and is staying at the Brown Palace Hotel. Be there at two o'clock."

When I arrived, on time, Joel ushered me into the suite; for the next hour together we enjoyed an exchange of information. He told me that he had been a personal friend of Master's and that Master had initiated him into Kriya Yoga. Master had also given him a key to his own quarters at the Encinitas hermitage so that Joel could have the use of them from time to time when Master was not in residence.

After talking for a while, we settled ourselves to meditate. Joel said, "You know, I have learned from many people, and I have practiced many meditation methods. These days, however, when I meditate, I just turn within and 'go unto the Father.'"

We meditated in silence, a silence with *presence*, and God's reality was evident. When our inner communion was established, Joel said, "You know, young man, your guru is right here with you!" He was overflowing with joy, so strong was the awareness. I had come to learn from him, and Joel was happy to meditate with me and to experience Master's love!

Later in the meeting, I asked him a personal question: "How does a person who has no organizational backing fund his ministry?" Joel was the ideal person to ask because for years he had traveled the world to teach classes and work with his students. While he was only too happy to cooperate with churches and organized groups, he never incorporated his work.

In response to my inquiry, he spread his arms expansively, smiled and exclaimed, "Why, Roy, it's all around you! All you have to do is reach out and take it!" As he spoke, a flash of insight surfaced in my consciousness and I was reminded that indeed, there is but One Presence, One Power, and One Substance, in and as this world—God. It took several years, however, for that insight to mature as experience.

Until his transition in 1964, Joel and I occasionally corresponded, and we met once or twice after our first meeting, when he visited Washington, D.C., where I occasionally lectured. I have always been pleased to recommend his books and publications. He was a person of integrity, and always followed the leading of the Spirit.

After Joel spoke one Sunday morning for a New Thought church, to a packed auditorium, the minister of that church said to me during a conversation, "Roy, you know I dearly love Joel, but I'll never again ask him to speak for our church."

"Why not?" I inquired. "People come in large numbers and his message is pure truth." I had been surprised at the minister's comment.

"What you say is true," she began, "but did you notice that he said that a person doesn't have to attend church in order to practice the presence of God?"

That was really the basis of the minister's problem: she felt that some of her members might stop attending church services as a result of Joel's comment.

Joel once told me in a letter that he felt that of all of his books, the three which best represented his mature thinking were *A Parenthesis in Eternity*, *The Contemplative Life*, and *The Thunder of Silence*.

After *The Thunder of Silence* was published in 1961, some New Thought ministers refused to have Joel as a guest speaker in their churches. The reason for this was his theme—that grace should rule our lives, that we should not overly strain to cause effects through prayer and mental imaging. The ministers, many of whom remained personal friends of Joel's, were teaching at the time the ideal of "making your world the way you want it to be," and they felt that Joel's message would confuse their members.

Joel made his transition in London, England, while on a teaching tour. He gave a talk one evening and, after it was over, handed the reel of audio tape to an assistant for later transcribing and said, "Well, I guess there's nothing more to say, is there?" He passed that night, in his hotel room.

Those who knew him remember him as an unswerving exponent of truth principles and a fully supportive teacher and friend. More and more, during his later years, he would quote Buddha and Shankara. At times during his travels, when there was no evening program scheduled, he would retire early, to awaken around midnight when the hotel was quiet, and meditate until dawn.

After a year of activity in Denver I realized that a large work was not destined to then unfold in that city, so I opened my mind to other possibilities. I was invited to speak for a group in Seattle, then for groups in Los Angeles. It was the beginning of ministry outreach.

In Los Angeles, I attended lectures by Neville Goddard, whose platform manner and presentation were always superb. Neville emphasized the importance of awakening spiritually, and the value of using controlled imagination to work in harmony with the mind of God. He had a marvelous sense of humor and embodied his teachings in his personal life.

Neville was born on the Caribbean island of Barbados. As a young man, he moved to New York City and became active in the theater as a dancer. During that time he met an Ethiopian rabbi to whom Neville referred only as "Abdullah." Neville became the rabbi's student and frequently visited him at his home in Harlem, cleaning his teacher's apartment in exchange for instruction. Neville used to tell the story of how, during that period of his life, he lived like an ascetic, eating no meat, having no social life, and spending most of his time in his apart-

Neville Goddard.

ment studying and meditating. One day his teacher said to him, "Neville, you're so good that you're good for nothing!" Then he said, "You are going to visit your family in Barbados. I see that when you return here you will have been reborn!"

Neville did visit his family in Barbados, and while there he did resume a more normal lifestyle. It happened without effort, and he began to once again appreciate and enjoy life.

He lectured in New York City for many years, drawing large audiences to his lectures, and writing books. He began to visit southern California from time to time, often sponsored by Dr. Frederick Bailes, then minister of a large Science of Mind church there. Dr. Bailes encouraged his friend to move to California. Finally, Neville did move there, and for several years he spoke twice a week in an art theater on Wilshire Boulevard in Los Angeles. It was there that I met him.

At that time I lived in a house in Los Angeles offered for my partial use by a chiropractor and psychologist, Dr. L. O. Anderson, who also encouraged me to use the large front room of the house for classes and seminars.

Realizing that I needed practical advice from successful truth teachers, I contacted several, and all were generous with their time and suggestions. It was in this way that I met and talked with Manly Palmer Hall, head of the Philosophical Research Society, author of many books and a lecturer with an incredible fund of information. Dr. Hall could speak on any metaphysical or esoteric subject for hours, without benefit of notes, and he could quote extensively from the great books of the world. A woman once approached him and said, "Dr. Hall, I know now how you are able to share so much with us when you speak. You have a spirit guide who provides you with the information!" Dr. Hall smiled and kindly said, "No, ma'am, I just happen to be extremely well read, and I just sit up there and think out loud."

The Philosophical Research Society, which is located in the Griffith Park district of Los Angeles, maintains offices, a lecture auditorium, and a most carefully assembled collection of rare books and manuscripts in its library.

Another useful visit was to the Science of Mind Institute,

where I enjoyed a delightful conversation with its founder, Ernest Holmes.

The first thing he said to me was, "I understand you're one of Yogananda's boys. He was a fine man." A pause, then he said, "If you had come in here a few minutes ago and seen me talking to myself you'd have thought I was out of my mind." Then he explained.

"I just got back from talking at some of our places in Florida. I met a man there who called me by telephone this morning and wanted me to pray for him. He had a problem, he said. So I sat here and began to "see" him improving. Then I caught myself and said, 'Ernest, don't be a darn fool! You don't believe that man has a problem, so why are you visualizing improvement?'"

Ernest's approach to praying for others was a technique he referred to as "spiritual mind treatment." In this technique, one first contemplates and feels the presence and reality of God. Since God is omnipresent, where the one who prays is, God is, and where the person in need of prayer is, God is. The person who has requested prayer is, in reality, a divine being. So the approach is to disregard the claim of a problem and just know the truth about the person. By renouncing the belief of limitation about another person, that person also experiences his belief in limitation dissolved, at least when the treatment is successfully experienced.

"I don't teach reincarnation, you know," Ernest told me. I responded, "I don't care if you do or not." He laughed and said, "I don't want people coming up to me and saying that they are going to wait until later to experience their good. I want them to learn to accept it here and now."

"And another thing," he went on, "I think it's a good idea to stay out of ruts, to be conscious all the time. For instance, the other day when I came into this office I purposely threw my hat on the chair and sat on the floor. And when I drive home at night I seldom take the same route two days in a row. I like to see things new all the time."

I next visited Dr. Ernest Wilson, then minister of the largest Unity congregation in the world. He also had known Paramahansaji, and he told me a story about Master. Many years before, while Dr. Wilson was still an independent truth teacher, he often traveled to major cities to lecture and conduct classes. When he arrived in Miami on one occasion, he learned that Master was scheduled to give a series of public talks on the same evenings that his own were scheduled. The advertising was underway and the halls were contracted for, so there was nothing left to do but go ahead with the programs.

Some people would attend Master's lectures one evening and Dr. Wilson's the next evening. One evening, Dr. Wilson noticed that a woman who was an every-other-night regular, and who always sat in the front row, was not present. The next day he received a telephone call from her. She was in the hospital with a fractured leg, and she asked Dr. Wilson to visit her, which he did. He asked her how it had happened.

"Well, you know I've been going to Swami's talks now and then. Last night, I would have been at your talk, but Swami was going to talk about healing and I didn't want to miss it. When he asked for volunteers from the audience to come to the stage for a demonstration I went forward. As you know, I'm pretty heavy and these steps going up to the stage just weren't made for a person as large as I am. I fell right through them! Now, Dr. Wilson, you tell me, why did that have to happen to me?"

Dr. Wilson jokingly said, "Well, my dear, I guess you were in the right place at the wrong time!" They had a good laugh over that comment, and the patient felt better.

I was later to visit with Dr. Wilson when he served as minister of Unity Temple in downtown Kansas City, Missouri. He was a very easy person to be with. Once, when I had just sat down in his office, he lit a cigarette and said to me, "I hope you're not a moralist! You know, there are some people who are so "spiritual" and with so much emphasis upon being "otherworldly" that one wonders if they even go to the bathroom as we mere mortals do!"

He told me some of the highlights of his ministry, and stressed the usefulness of practicing a technique he had learned from Emmet Fox. Dr. Fox at one time attracted in New York

City the largest congregation of any church in the world, numbering over 9,000 people. Ernest said, "When I go to sleep every night, I see myself, in my mind's eye, standing before throngs of people, all of whom are joyously receiving my message of truth. When a person does this, you know, it has to reflect outwardly in this world."

He also shared a personal experience: "Sometimes when I'm speaking in the pulpit I feel myself expanding until I am larger than my body, sort of hovering over it, yet conscious that the body is speaking. During such times I am aware of the needs of the people in the congregation, as well as being able to have access to anecdotes and scriptural references which will perfectly meet their needs. Somehow it all comes together. Then, when I finish the sermon or the class I feel myself coming back into the body. I don't know how it's done, but it just happens now and again."

During that time in Los Angeles I felt like a small fish in a huge body of water. There were so many beautifully effective truth teachers in southern California and I still felt young and inexperienced. Small groups of dedicated devotees would gather with me for classes, but I was not able to attract large numbers of people.

A few months before I left Los Angeles I met Walter C. Lanyon, a delightful man and, as he himself freely admitted, more than a little eccentric. Walter was born in England of American parents. He had traveled the world over, missing very little of what it had to offer, so he said. Standing not more than five feet tall, and in his late seventies or early eighties when I met him, he seemed almost to be a prankish elf. His general appearance was that of an elderly man who could have used the help of someone to look after him, to make sure his shoes were shined and his necktie straight.

Walter had studied Christian Science, among other things, and could play the piano, and discuss art and literature knowledgeably. Now and then he went on a binge of impressionist oil painting. He called it "messing around" and the results were proof, but the paintings sold to his friends, who happened to love anything Walter did. When he was not

writing and lecturing on truth principles, he would write
novels and travel books under another name. In that way,
when he felt like withdrawing from the public eye, he could
still earn enough money to meet his needs.

I had written to him in care of his publisher, De Vorss &
Company, a distributor of metaphysical books then based in
Los Angeles. A few days later, while washing the breakfast
dishes, I looked out the window and observed a white Cadillac
coupe come to a stop across the street. Its occupant emerged,
crossed the street, and soon the doorbell rang. When I opened
the door Walter said, "Are you Roy Eugene? I'm Walter Lanyon." His unannounced arrival was, I came to learn, characteristic of Walter. He was a spontaneous person.

He told me a story during our first meeting. He had been,
he said, driving to San Diego once a week to speak for a large
Religious Science church, where about 800 persons gathered
weekly to hear him. The previous week he had driven to the
church and, fifteen minutes into his talk, had discovered that
he had nothing more to say on that occasion. He simply said
to the audience, "That's it! See you next week!" He then
walked to his car and drove back to Los Angeles. The following
week the auditorium was full to overflowing, because everyone wanted to see this unpredictable speaker!

One day, after we had lunched together, he looked at me
and said, "When I look at you I see this inner light in your
breast. I have the gift, you know. I can see things. You have
this inner light and seem to be holding it in. Why don't you
let it out?"

I knew what he was talking about. I have always been a
shy person. In high school I nearly failed a public speaking
course because I was so nervous about standing up in front of
the small group of classmates. Oral book reports, when an
assignment was given to me, would result in sleepless nights.
Even today, when I walk to the podium to address an audience
of perhaps a thousand or more, sometimes the thought, "What
am I doing here?" floats into my mind.

I have no problem talking about God and how to know

Him. I have nothing new to say; I can only tell the old, old story—and I love to tell that story.

"You need experience," Walter continued. "Just travel around the country and get some experience!"

"Where should I go?" I retorted. "I'm not known and I don't have any money to use for that kind of thing."

Walter became serious and, fixing me with his eyes, said, "What would Jesus say to that? Go! Go, now! Everything will be provided. You will see. But you must go." Pausing for a moment, to be still and reflect, he said, "Everything is waiting for you. Go, now."

That evening I wrote a letter to Dr. Gilbert Holloway, then minister of the New Age Church of Truth in Miami, Florida. I offered to speak for a two-week "truth crusade" series. Gilbert promptly responded to my letter, and we entered into an agreement.

After arrangements had been made, and before I left Los Angeles for Miami, Walter and I met by chance near a supermarket where I had gone to shop for food. He pretended surprise, assumed a pose reminiscent of gunfighters about to "shoot it out," and challenged, "What are you still doing here? I told you to get out of town!"

We then talked for a few minutes while I explained my plans. He was happy for me, and even attended my seminar on the following weekend, "just to check me out," he later told me.

When I arrived in Miami, in that spring of 1958, an interview was scheduled with the religion editor of the *Miami Herald*; two days later the morning edition carried a story. On Sunday morning the modest church auditorium was filled. I was scheduled to speak twice on Sundays and four nights a week, for the two-week series. The response was so positive that when Dr. Holloway left on his annual lecture tour at the end of the two weeks, he asked me to stay and continue the meetings for another month. During the six weeks I was there I gave almost forty lectures, and was frequently asked to counsel individuals and to give private instruction. Radio interviews were also given, usually on one of the late night talk shows which were then so popular.

An interesting episode occurred when I first arrived in Miami. During our initial conversation, Dr. Holloway asked, "You give readings, don't you? I hope so, because we've already announced that you would, and many people have already asked for an appointment."

I had met one or two psychics the year before, and knew about readings, but I was not much attracted to the idea of offering them. When I explained my feelings to Dr. Holloway, he said, "I'm sure you can do it. I'll tell you what. A lady is coming in this afternoon to talk with me and I know she won't mind if you sit in and observe. Just watch how I do it and you'll pick it up."

During the appointment, as I observed, I found that impressions would float to the surface of my mind, and that a moment or two later, Dr. Holloway would verbalize them. He was right; I could do it.

During the remainder of my stay in Miami I gave readings, and everyone who had an appointment with me seemed satisfied. I continued to offer readings through the summer months while speaking in Washington, D.C., Philadelphia, and New York City. I didn't refer to them as readings, but as "intuitive counseling sessions." I found that I could sit with a total stranger, instruct him not to tell me anything about himself until I had finished, then meditate and begin to talk. I would mentally see their past, their present conditions, and their possible future if they chose not to change mental attitude or behavior. I would pick up trivial details, also, such as the color of their automobile, how their house or apartment was decorated, the names of their pets and, of course, some of their secret fantasies.

My routine was to talk for about fifteen minutes, to assure them that I had insight, and then begin to ask them about their goals and purposes and encourage them to find solutions to their problems. Then I taught them to meditate.

It was a phase for me; I didn't like being thought of as a psychic and I cared less for the fact that the majority of the

Father Divine.

people who came to me were not willing to assume personal responsibility for their thoughts and actions. To most of them I was merely another fortune teller. After some months, even though I continued to be available to sincere seekers, I discontinued giving readings.

While speaking in several cities during the summer of 1958 I accepted invitations from various groups: psychology forums, New Age churches, a few spiritualist churches, and even a flying saucer club. I considered myself a missionary, and I would go wherever I was asked, but my message was never diluted and I did not allow myself to become involved with activities with which I did not feel comfortable.

One morning, while visiting Philadelphia to keep a lecture engagement, I thought of Father Divine. Opening the telephone directory, I noted that the main office of his organization, the Peace Mission Movement, was located only a few blocks from my hotel, at Broad and Catherine Streets. Shortly after noon I walked up to an imposing building and felt inclined to ring the doorbell. An elderly gentleman opened the door and welcomed me with a smile. Behind him I could see the large main room, filled with men and women who were sitting at long banquet tables. At the head table sat Father Divine. He looked at me across the room and smiled a welcome. "Show the young gentleman in," he said.

I was led to within fifteen feet of where Father Divine sat and was provided a chair and a glass of water. There were no vacant places at the tables. From time to time Father looked at me and smiled his beautiful smile, his eyes revealing his spiritual qualities. I felt drawn to stand up and say something to him but I resisted the urge. Finally he stood, welcomed everyone, and invited anyone who felt inclined to speak to do so freely. Then he looked at me again and smiled. The force of his spiritual power was overwhelming. I was literally pulled to my feet by it, and managed to express my appreciation to him. I reminded him of our correspondence two years before, and conveyed Walter Lanyon's regards to him.

Many years before our meeting, Walter had carried on a lengthy correspondence with Father Divine; later he quoted extensively from those letters in two of his books. In Walter's book *The Eyes of the Blind*, we find these words, written by Father Divine:

> I am thinking of the things of Spirit that are made flesh, and how the Spirit spiritualizes them. Therefore Spirit materialized is incorruptible, undefiled and fadeth not away. Hence, being Spirit, I am happy, I am free. Nothing can or does hold me, for I am Spirit, even though I am flesh. Yet in my flesh do I see God. My eyes see Him for myself.
>
> Jesus did not advocate gifts, He advocated the giver. He did not advocate blessings, He advocated the blesser.
>
> All mortal habits, systems, ways, ideas, etc., are weights. When you have thrown off the weight and the sin—which does so easily beset you—then you will run the race that is set before you, and wait patiently for Christ to rise in you. Cast all mortal tendencies, personal ideas and fancies, out of your consciousness, and consequently out of your system, and you will suddenly experience a feeling of lightness. You will feel like a new creature. It is wonderful to know that when you have made the complete surrender and sacrifice all these human beliefs and tendencies, that Christ is risen in you. Just as soon as you make the complete surrender He will rise instantaneously. It is wonderful.

During his time on earth Father Divine's teachings and personal example lifted hundreds of thousands of people. He stressed the spiritual essence of every person, and taught people how to live honest and purposeful lives. During the Great Depression in the United States in the 1930's, he fed thousands of people free daily meals. He encouraged his followers to band together and form cooperative communities so that they could pool their resources and experience a higher standard of living. He absolutely would not tolerate words or actions by his followers which were prejudiced. Men and women of many races and nationalities gathered together with him and learned to experience true brotherhood.

While sitting in the main room of the headquarters building that day, I was suddenly struck with the fact that I had been in the room before. Then I remembered that a year or two before, while experiencing a conscious dream, I had been in that room and had seen Father Divine come into it.

At another time, following a lecture in Philadelphia, a woman approached me and related the following experience. Years before, a friend of hers had invited her to attend a meeting where Father Divine would be present. She reluctantly agreed to meet her friend later that evening at the meeting hall. That afternoon, she felt ill and retired to her bedroom to sleep for a while. As she slept she dreamed that she saw the face of a kindly man who looked into her eyes and smiled at her. When she awakened she no longer felt ill. When she entered the meeting hall that evening and saw Father Divine, she recognized him as the person who had smiled at her in her dream.

Years after I met him, I learned from a news broadcast on television that Father Divine had made his transition. His body was placed in a beautiful shrine on the grounds of an estate owned by the Peace Mission Movement. His spirit continues to nourish his many followers around the world. His wife, Mother Divine, succeeded him as organizational head of the movement, but to her, and to the members, Father will always be the head of the movement.

The following anecdote may serve to give an indication of how far-reaching his influence has been. The year after he had moved from the visible to the Invisible, I was talking with two men who were police officers in Miami, Florida. They regularly attended my lectures when I was in that city, and we sometimes would share lunch or dinner together. They told me of a then recent incident which had taken place in Miami Beach at one of the resort hotels. A hotel guest had reported the theft of her jewelry, and many people who were employed by the hotel had been questioned by police investigators. One man, while being questioned, happened to mention that he was a follower of Father Divine. The officer in charge immediately apologized to him and said, "Let him go. If he is a follower of Father Divine he couldn't have done it. Father Divine's followers are honest!"

One evening in Philadelphia, while I was preparing to enter the chapel where I was to speak, a woman approached me and asked, "Would you like to be on television tonight?" She explained that she represented a local station and was responsible for arranging guests for a late night talk show hosted by Joe Pyne. I had not heard of Mr. Pyne at the time, and I readily agreed.

The Joe Pyne Show was, for a few years in the early 1960's, one of the most controversial programs aired. When I first went on his show he was just beginning to build his reputation as a "tough" interviewer. That's a very mild description!

This particular show, however, went very well. Joe had had a guest cancellation and needed a replacement. He debated with me just enough to keep his audience happy and, during station breaks, was friendly and supportive. He also generously announced my lecture engagement in that city. The next night the chapel was overflowing with interested people, and I realized then the extent of the influence of television.

A few years later, in 1964, when Joe Pyne had become nationally known, was on the air five times a week broadcasting over more than seventy radio stations throughout the country, and was based in Hollywood, California, I was again asked to be on his show. I readily agreed.

When I arrived at the studio he was relaxed and cheerful. "Hi, Roy," he began. "I remember you from that last time in Philadelphia—it was a good interview. This time I've got a problem. . .I've had a guest cancel out and instead of doing one thirty-minute show I'd like you to stay a little longer and do two programs. Is that all right with you?" Of course, it was fine with me, and both sessions went well. He was then recording two or three interviews a day for later broadcast.

A few months later, after I had returned from visiting Japan, where I spoke in several cities, I was again asked to be

Speaking in Chicago during a conference sponsored by the Universal Foundation for Better Living, Inc., Dr. Johnnie Colemon, founder.

on his show. Though he was not as amiable as before, the interview was worthwhile because of his increased audience.

More television shows were also included in my schedule, usually morning variety programs broadcast locally, although occasionally I would appear on a show with national coverage. Public response to lectures was not always dramatic as the result of radio or television exposure, but it was useful experience and an easy way to reach thousands of people with a few words of positive help.

Radio talk shows proliferated, and I appeared on well over one hundred such shows in various cities, during the period 1958 to 1964. I was always visiting a different city, I was a published author by then, and an American teacher of Yoga. As Morgan Beatty of NBC Radio once said after we had been on the air for an hour one weekend, "Come back anytime; you're a good interview." That was his way of saying, "You hold up your end of the conversation and what you say interests the listeners."

Some very interesting interview experiences were with Long John Nebel. For years, his program was broadcast from midnight until 5 A.M. from the studios of WOR Radio in New York City. Long John, as he advertised himself, could sell almost anything. When I met him he was known for having guests on his show whose unusual claims and stories challenged and entertained the listening audience. Sometimes he would interview a local politician, or people involved in a currently newsworthy cause. Often he would have as his guests psychics, mediums, flying saucer contactees, tarot card readers, New Thought teachers and, of course, a yogi now and then. Dr. Gilbert Holloway was a frequent guest on the program when he was in town. It was he who recommended me to Mr. Nebel as a possible guest. Gilbert was very generous in this way, and I still remember his kindnesses with deep appreciation.

The first time I was interviewed on the Long John Show was during a two-week lecture series in Manhattan at the Steinway Concert Hall on 57th Street. I had given only the first few lectures, and audiences had not been large. The afternoon following my appearance on Long John, however, there were people standing, because all of the seats were taken. I talked with a young man after the lecture and asked him how he had heard of the lecture meeting. His response was interesting. "Last night I was in my room at the YMCA and couldn't sleep and didn't have anything else to do, so I carried some trash down to the waste bin behind the building. There I saw a broken radio someone had thrown away and I thought, 'I'll just see if I can fix that.' I took it upstairs and played with it awhile and it started working. The first thing I heard was, 'This is Long John Nebel, and our guest tonight is Roy Eugene Davis, an American who is a yogi, and who will be speaking in our town tomorrow.' That's why I'm here. And I'm glad I'm here. Thank you."

During my visits to east coast cities during this period, I made available to those who gathered at the lectures a collection of class notes. I titled the collection, *Come Ye Out*. The theme was to "come out from human consciousness and experience the clear light of understanding." When the first mimeographed edition sold out I decided to have the material typeset and published as a hardbound book.

I took the manuscript to a printer and asked for a quote. I was told that it would cost $1,200 to pay for typesetting, printing and binding. I asked for some time to think about the matter and returned to my hotel room. I had but a third of the amount needed in my checking account. The plant manager had told me that if I wanted to, I could pay in three equal installments as the work progressed.

While pondering my decision, I happened to be reading a copy of one of Walter Lanyon's books, *Thrust in the Sickle*. He had chosen the title after reading *Joel 3:13* in the Old Testament: "Put ye in the sickle, for the harvest is ripe." A sickle is a sharp curved blade used to cut stalks of grain. I was suddenly struck with the thought, "What am I waiting for? The fact that I had the idea to publish means that, in God's mind, it is already published!"

I called the printer and entered into an agreement. Then, putting a check in an envelope as partial payment, I sent it to the printing plant. Two weeks later the typeset proofs were delivered. By then I was able to make a second payment; I began to announce that the book would soon be available. Two weeks after that the bound books were delivered, and I had enough money in hand to pay the final bill.

The first edition of one thousand copies sold rapidly. Adding a few more chapters to the text, I changed the title to *Time, Space and Circumstance* and arranged for a printing of three thousand copies. A year later, these had been distributed, but I was finding out that it was a challenge for me to travel and lecture, at the same time overseeing a modest publishing venture. What to do? Well, one does the obvious!

During this time I was staying at the Great Northern Hotel in New York City, just across the street from Steinway Concert Hall, where my meetings were scheduled. I had three more days of lectures in Manhattan before moving on to Philadelphia, where a two-week series of talks was already being publicized. It was early in the morning and I had dressed and was preparing to go out to a nearby restaurant for breakfast. A statement came into my mind and I verbalized it: I *spoke the word* with conviction: "Before I leave this city I will find the right publisher, one who is right for me, and my books right for him!" Then I released the matter from my conscious mind.

At a corner newsstand in front of Carnegie Hall, I stopped to purchase a morning paper. While waiting for my change, I casually leafed through a magazine which happened to be convenient. On the inside back cover I saw a full-page advertisement offering a self-help book. I had not until then heard of the publisher, whose name and address were included in the advertisement. On impulse, I purchased the magazine and then went on to the restaurant. After placing my order, I went to the telephone and called the publisher's office.

I was put through immediately to the president of the company, Mr. Frederick Fell, of Frederick Fell, Inc. After a few minutes of conversation, he invited me to visit him at his offices.

Fred and I talked for a while and he told me that he had only recently started to publish self-help and motivational books. Before that he had specialized in novels and biographies. I left a copy of *Time, Space and Circumstance* with him, along with a recently completed manuscript for another book, and returned to my hotel. Later that afternoon, Fred telephoned me and said, "Roy, I'll take them both!"

So just a few hours after experiencing a clear realization, a mutually useful business transaction was agreed upon. I had contacted a few other publishers earlier, but none of them had wanted to take a chance on an unknown writer.

I was now free to devote all my energies to ministering and writing, my publisher taking care of book distribution. I traveled to at least twenty cities a year, to lecture and conduct weekend seminars. When not traveling I handled correspondence, initiated a series of monthly lessons for my students, and wrote three more books.

For some time I had felt a personal need to more closely examine the inner meaning of Patanjali's *Yoga Sutras*. What better way to study the material than to write a commentary on it? Obtaining two or three translations of the work by other authors, I set about the project of paraphrasing the English translations from the Sanskrit and writing a commentary in plain English which would be understood by those who came to my meetings, most of whom were students in the New Thought tradition but with little experience or contact with the science and philosophy of Yoga.

The *Yoga Sutras* explain the way of liberation of consciousness as the result of eradicating inner restricting tendencies and influences. Living in harmony with the order of the universe is emphasized, along with meditation procedures and inner perceptions. When the manuscript was completed, I titled it *This Is Reality* and had it published in a limited edition of five hundred copies. Since then it has been distributed in various editions, including one in the German language. Years later I again wrote a commentary on this scripture and published it under the title, *The Science of Kriya Yoga*. In this latter treatment I related the teaching to the practice of the Kriya Yoga techniques and procedures.

While writing *This Is Reality* I experienced a deep inner

attunement with my guru line. I particularly thought about Sri Yukteswar, Paramahansaji's guru, because he was known for his keen intellectual powers, and doing a commentary on the *Yoga Sutras* certainly called for discernment. One night I dreamed of Sri Yukteswar. It was a vivid experience. We were standing at the foot of Mt. Washington in Los Angeles, and we put our arms around each other and began to climb the wooden stairway. I will not here attempt an interpretation of the symbolism of that dream. Even today, the memory of climbing the stairs, holding in my arms my spiritual grandfather, whom I never met in the flesh, is precious.

The veil between outer and inner realms is very nebulous. Some sensitive souls can easily move in awareness from one realm to another. There are those who can see into subtle realms through spiritual eye perception. There are those, too, who know what is taking place anywhere in the universe, in any sphere or dimension, merely by being open to that knowing. They know their omnipresence, and that everything created is contained within them.

It was while on a lecture tour of Florida cities that I had my first conscious out-of-the-body experience. It took place a few days after President John Kennedy was assassinated in Dallas. I was in St. Petersburg when I heard the news on the car radio, and attendance at my lecture that night was small because many people were numb with shock over the incident.

In Orlando I stayed with friends who had invited me to be their house guest. After eating lunch and having talked for a while, it was mutually decided that we would rest for a while in order to be at our best during the lecture planned for that evening.

Going to my room, I closed the door and reclined on the bed to rest. My body was tired and I was soon experiencing a reverie state, during which I was still conscious but inwardly turned. I could hear Bryant moving about in the living room, and his wife, Helen, in the bathroom. I could hear the water running in the shower. Without premeditation I experienced that I was floating straight up, still in a horizontal position. I opened my eyes to see the ceiling about six inches from my face. It seemed perfectly natural to be doing this so I "rolled over" and looked down at my physical body on the bed. Then I thought, "I wonder if I can see through walls?" I could still hear Bryant in the adjacent living room. I tried to look through the door and, as I did so, I felt myself descend, head first, into my physical form. I opened my eyes and looked around, then reminded myself to remember the incident and went to sleep.

When I awoke, two or more hours later, I experienced a dull ache at the base of my skull. I was mentally alert and felt rested, but for the rest of the day that minor dull ache at the base of the skull remained.

That evening, over a light meal, I told Bryant and Helen of my experience. Helen laughed and said, "You know, after you went to your room and I stepped into the shower I had this thought, 'I wonder if Roy can see through walls?'"

Over the years, during interludes of reverie, I have spontaneously experienced other-dimensional perceptions, seen through walls, observed Planet Earth from a vantage point in distant space, and known direct inner communication with people who inhabit this world and worlds existing in a different space-time continuum than ours.

During the early 1960's I lived in Maryland, near Washington, D.C. When not traveling I frequently spoke at the Church of Divine Science. Dr. Grace Faus, a conscientious truth teacher and extremely thoughtful lady, was then minister of the church. She generously offered her pulpit to other ministers; Dr. Joseph Murphy and Dr. Frederick Bailes were two of the more popular who visited.

During one of Dr. Bailes' visits, church attendance was small because snow had fallen earlier in the day. The next night, the snow having melted, the sanctuary was filled. Dr. Bailes commented, "I've always taught that what a person experiences is the result of his state of consciousness. Last night, when I saw only a few people here, I almost gave up the ministry!" Everyone enjoyed the humorous way he handled the incident.

For two consecutive summers, while Dr. Faus vacationed in her beloved Colorado, I was asked to conduct Sunday services and midweek classes at the church. Because she felt that some of her members would feel more comfortable having an ordained Divine Science minister in the pulpit, she asked if I would accept ordination in that church. It was understood that I would in no way be obligated to change my teaching emphasis or method of presentation. I accepted her proposal, flew to Denver to meet the executive board of the headquarters church, and was later ordained by Dr. Gregg, then president of the federation of Divine Science churches.

Until this time my ministry had not yet extended beyond the borders of the United States, except through the printed word. However, events would soon transpire which would result in circumstances which would be the beginning of a world-wide ministry.

SIX

Journey to Japan

Whenever I went to New York City I would make it a point to visit Inspiration House, a bookstore owned and operated by Eden Gray. She always stocked the latest titles, with emphasis on the books of Joel S. Goldsmith, Neville, Walter Lanyon (some of whose titles she published), and other New Thought writers.

Eden had had a successful career as an actress, mostly on the stage, and she was also a licensed Religious Science practitioner. She often sponsored speakers when they visited New York City, as well as interviewing them on her daily radio show, which featured authors and books. It was through her that I met Dr. Raymond Charles Barker, then minister of First Church of Religious Science, and Dr. Paul Brunet, who was minister of another Religious Science church in the city. One day in 1963, Dr. Brunet gave me a copy of a book by Dr. Masaharu Taniguchi. It was to prove to be one of those special connections that make a difference.

As I read Dr. Taniguchi's book, I was impressed with his clear teaching, emphasizing that "man is a child of God and can live in a world of Reality, in which sickness and limitations cannot exist." I noted, in the appended material, that Dr.

Taniguchi's organization, *Seicho-No-Ie* (Home of Infinite Life, Wisdom and Abundance), had a publishing department which published not only his books but those of other authors. Out of gratitude for his having written the book that I had just finished reading, I sent him a personal letter and an autographed copy of *Time, Space and Circumstance.*

A few months later I received a letter from the International Department of Seicho-No-Ie in Tokyo, requesting my assistance. Dr. Taniguchi was planning his first world tour. Most of the arrangements were being coordinated through Founder's Church of Religious Science in Los Angeles, but a problem had come up regarding Dr. Taniguchi's planned visit to New York City.

I made a quick telephone call to Dr. Brunet in New York to explain the situation, and Dr. Brunet contacted the New York Unity Center, which readily agreed to sponsor Dr. Taniguchi's talks there. Another telephone call to Dr. Faus and two evenings were scheduled for Washington, D.C.

Dr. Taniguchi's tour was a great success, with hundreds attending in most cities. From North America he went on to Europe, and then to South America, where on one occasion over 30,000 people gathered in a stadium to hear him. His work has continued to be strong in South America, particularly in Brazil, where well over 300,000 members are involved.

When Dr. Taniguchi and his party arrived at the airport for their stay in Washington, D.C., they were met by myself, Dr. Faus and some of her church members, and by representatives of the Japanese Embassy. Dr. Faus' son-in-law, James Goure, arranged a special luncheon in a restaurant at the Pentagon, where he was employed. I was seated to Dr. Taniguchi's right, and we talked during lunch.

"How would you like to come to Japan?" he said, with a broad smile. "Come next year, in September, and we will publish your book there in Japanese translation and arrange for you to speak in several cities."

I didn't hesitate in giving my assent. The dates mentioned by Dr. Taniguchi were over a year away, so I would have ample time to prepare for the visit to Japan.

While continuing my regular duties I held, in the background of my mind, the "perfect picture" of a successful trip to Japan. Correspondence flowed back and forth as plans became firm. I arranged, far ahead of time, a visit to California cities just prior to my scheduled departure date from Los Angeles to Tokyo. During the summer of 1964 I spoke frequently in San Diego and Los Angeles, with a brief visit to San Francisco also included.

My first lecture in the Los Angeles area was in Grauman's Chinese Theater in Hollywood, where the Hollywood Science of Mind Church held Sunday services. Dr. Harry Douglas Smith, who had formerly been an associate minister with Dr. Frederick Bailes, was then minister of the Hollywood church. All of the lectures and seminars offered at other times during that summer in the Los Angeles area were held at the Hollywood Knickerbocker Hotel. Hollywood was at that time still a popular tourist stop and the glamour made real by legends had not yet dimmed.

What a welcome I met as my Japan Airlines plane taxied to a stop at the airport near Tokyo! Looking out of the window I could see at least fifty people standing on the terminal roof, waving small Japanese and American flags. When I disembarked I was met by Reverend Tamura and other representatives of Seicho-No-Ie. Everyone was smiling and waving and pressing close to shake my hand. In the lobby of the terminal, with everything beautifully orchestrated, yet allowing for any spontaneous happening, photographers gathered to take pictures, and many gorgeous flower bouquets were heaped into my arms.

I was taken by car to the Tobitakyu Spiritual Training School near Tokyo and shown to a private room just off the hallway leading to the lecture room. The facility, a former army hospital, had been purchased after the Second World War. It was intended for use as a maternity hospital, where women who wanted the option of having a natural delivery for their infants could go, but the government would not allow such a hospital at that time. The doctor who was to have been in charge, Dr. Katsumi Tokuhisa, had already given up his

Official photo of Dr. Masaharu Taniguchi taken shortly before his transition. *Courtesy, Seicho-No-Ie International Department, Tokyo.*

practice in Manchuria. He became a minister of Seicho-No-Ie and the director of the Spiritual Training School which was started there.

Every courtesy was shown me. I was taken on a sightseeing tour of Tokyo which included the national championship *sumo* wrestling contests. Dinners were arranged, where I met with Dr. Taniguchi and members of the Seicho-No-Ie executive board, as well as various department heads.

The first scheduled lecture took place in Tokyo on a Monday afternoon. I asked my interpreter, the Reverend Haruo Shibuya, if people would attend a public lecture scheduled at such a time. He laughed and said, "Anytime Dr. Taniguchi speaks, the people will come. You will see."

Two thousand people filled the auditorium. Huge flags, one American and one Japanese, dominated the stage backdrop. Both national anthems were played, and special people were introduced. Dr. Taniguchi formally welcomed me to Japan and presented me with a copy of one of his books, a copy of my book in Japanese translation, and a certificate and lapel pin designating me an honorary minister of Seicho-No-Ie.

I was then introduced, and I delivered a prepared lecture. Dr. Taniguchi then spoke. The entire program lasted almost four hours.

In the remainder of the cities on that tour, I was to experience similar programs. Dr. Taniguchi did not accompany me on the tour; my traveling companions were Dr. Tokuhisa and Reverend Shibuya. At each stop we would meet with the welcoming organizational representatives, visit local temples and shrines, participate in the afternoon lecture program, rest for a while, and then have our evening meal in a specially chosen restaurant. We traveled from city to city by train, giving us an opportunity to see the countryside as we went.

When the tour was over, we stayed for one night in a hotel near the base of Mt. Fuji, expecting to enjoy a good view of that revered mountain the following morning. Alas, with the breaking of day there was such heavy fog that the mountain could not be seen. From there we went to Yokohama and then back to Tokyo.

On the final full day in Japan I was taken, along with several others, to Dr. Taniguchi's Tokyo residence for lunch. Prior to the meal, while talking with some of the ministers and directors present, the man who was then president of the publishing firm asked me a question. I had been informed that he was well known in Japan for his books on zen buddhism. "Does the world exist?" he asked me abruptly. I had read material on zen and was not overly surprised or challenged by the question. Pausing before answering, I said, "No, the world does not exist." I noted that the others in the group relaxed. My answer had been the correct one.

Of course, what the gentleman was really asking me was, "Does the material universe have independent reality?" Of course, it does not. Matter is but another form of energy, and energy flows from the Godhead, and the Godhead is the initial outward expression of Supreme Consciousness. Therefore, the material worlds cannot have independent existence.

I was pleasantly surprised upon my arrival at the airport the following day to again see dozens of Seicho-No-Ie members gathered, this time to wish me bon voyage. Dr. and Mrs. Taniguchi were also there, a gesture which touched everyone deeply.

A few days later, after my arrival in Los Angeles, I was asked to speak at the North American Headquarters Church of Seicho-No-Ie, located in Gardena, not far from downtown Los Angeles. I reported on the visit to Japan and shared with the audience a film which had been given to me by Dr. Tokuhisa, showing the highlights of the tour.

While in Japan, I had asked Dr. Taniguchi for permission to write his biography for English-reading people, a proposal to which he readily agreed. This book was eventually published both in America and Japan under the title, *Miracle Man of Japan*. It has since been used by all Seicho-No-Ie centers as an introduction to Dr. Taniguchi's teachings for non-Japanese speaking inquirers.

Among the publicly known spiritual leaders of Japan, Dr. Taniguchi was one of the better known and more influential of the current century. He embarked upon an enlightenment quest at an early age. Like many before him, he asked the basic questions: Why do people suffer and experience poverty? Why are some people exploited, while others seem to live a charmed life? What is the meaning of it all? He read widely and examined the great scriptures of the world, including those of Buddhism and Christianity.

One day in a bookstore he came across a copy of *The Law of Mind in Action* by Fenwicke Holmes, a brother of Ernest Holmes. Here was the key that caused everything in his mind to come together. He read that the universal mental law enables a person to attract whatever he believes he should have, and that the phenomenal world is but a reflection of one's mental states and states of consciousness.

Meditating daily, Dr. Taniguchi experienced revelation after revelation. It sometime seemed that an inner voice provided answers to his questions. One revelation was:

All things evolve from nothingness and take form according to thought patterns. You suffer because you believe matter to be real and solid. Your soul will be emancipated from all restriction and obtain freedom if you do not adhere to matter by believing it to be real. See it for what it is. Infinite supply will come. You can draw out infinitude from nothingness and have plenty left over. The phenomenal world is merely a temporal manifestation of an illusory mental picture seen through the lens of the mind. It has no existence of its own.

Again he inquired and the revelation came:

The void is not the true state of Reality. Things of the phenomenal world are all nothingness and material things and mental phases are all vanity. The five principles of matter, senses, cognition, will, and consciousness, are all vanity! You stumble because you do not know that all five principles are delusion. Things manifest as real when you cognize them. The true essence of Reality is God. Only God exists. The things that are real are only the Mind of God, and the manifestations

Dr. and Mrs. Taniguchi seeing me off at the Japan Airlines
terminal, Tokyo, Japan, September, 1964.

Reverend Haruo Shibuya translates for me as I address a large audience near Kyoto, Japan.

of the Mind of God. By denying all illusory appearances on the physical plane you can know the real
God, the real Buddha (the enlightened nature). Realize
this truth! Immortal life will be restored here and now!
Now! The eternal now! Resurrection is now! Live the
now!

Opening himself to his good, he soon obtained a well paid
position. In his free time he began to write articles, and he
published a small magazine to share with friends. So great was
the response that before long he had to resign from his job in
order to keep up with the demands for his time as a counselor
and truth teacher. Gradually his ministry unfolded, as it met
the needs of multiplied thousands of people. It would, in time,
grow to such proportions that over three million copies of
Seicho-No-Ie magazine would be published and distributed
monthly, and Dr. Taniguchi's basic set of truth books would
sell over twenty million copies. He authored other books, too,
hundreds of them. He toured the major cities of Japan, and
thousands would pack the largest auditoriums for his lecture
series. Churches and centers were formed, ministers were
trained, the mighty work prospered, and it continues to prosper to this day.

One reason for the popularity of Seicho-No-Ie's teaching
ministry is that, while there is much to challenge the intellect,
emphasis has always been placed on helping people to experience solutions to their problems as a result of awakening to
the realization of their true nature.

In 1978, I again toured Japan at the invitation of Dr. Taniguchi. Interpreting for me in various cities were Reverend
Shibuya, Reverend Tamura, and Reverend Masayo Tsuruta,
who had translated my book, *Studies in Truth*, to be made
available at the lectures.

After a night's rest in Tokyo, we went by train to Kyoto
to visit some Shinto shrines and Buddhist temples, then on to
Seicho-No-Ie's shrine at nearby Uji. I had been there in 1972
for a day or two to rest, but this time over 6,000 members had
gathered to participate in a weekend program. Dr. Taniguchi

and others were on the platform when we arrived. Thousands were gathered in the main hall, and a nearby building provided closed-circuit television viewing for the overflow audience. I was asked to speak that afternoon, which I did, with the able assistance of Reverend Shibuya. The audience was most loving and responsive, as has been my experience with audiences whenever I have spoken in Japan.

Before visiting the remaining cities on that tour, we went to the Grand Shrine of Seicho-No-Ie near Nagasaki. Here, several hundred acres of wooded mountain land had been purchased. The central focus was to be a huge meeting hall and a modern hotel-style building to be used for spiritual training intensives. The grounds had not yet been dedicated at the time, and final touches were being applied to the grounds and the buildings. The land development and building projects had taken seven years to complete, at a cost of twenty million dollars, all of the support coming from Seicho-No-Ie members.

The last time I saw Dr. Taniguchi was at his home near the Grand Shrine. He had moved there to be in semi-retirement, but still, I was told, maintained an exacting daily schedule of meditation and writing. He was due to arrive from Kyoto, and several ministers and department heads invited me to join them as a welcoming party. When his car came to a stop he eased himself out and stood. We shook hands warmly. He looked up at me, turned to the others, smiled broadly and exclaimed, "He's so *tall*!"

Two or three of us then followed him into his house and sat with him in the living room. He had settled himself on a large couch, Mrs. Taniguchi at his side. His body had become more frail since I had last seen him, and he moved more slowly. Clasping my hands in his with a strong grip, he said, "The body is a little tired now, but the spirit is strong."

In June, 1985, a telephone message was conveyed to me by a secretary in the CSA office. A representative of the Gardena Seicho-No-Ie church had called to inform me that Dr. Taniguchi had made his transition the day before, on June 17. A few days later, a letter from Reverend Shibuya was delivered, sharing more details.

Dr. Taniguchi had entered a hospital in Nagasaki and, after a few days, there passed from his body. The following afternoon a private funeral service was conducted at his former residence, for family members and a few close friends. Formal services were conducted at the Grand Shrine on July 22nd. Many thousands of Seicho-No-Ie members and friends were in attendance.

As soon as we were informed of his passing, I requested that a large framed photograph of Dr. Taniguchi be placed near the altar in the CSA Meditation Hall. Fresh roses were placed before the photograph throughout the rest of June, and regular prayers were offered on his behalf.

Reverend Seicho Taniguchi, Dr. Taniguchi's son-in-law, succeeded him as head of the movement. Because of Reverend Seicho Taniguchi's capable leadership, and the dedication of many superbly trained ministers and teachers, the dynamic service of Seicho-No-Ie will continue.

Dr. Taniguchi was in his ninety-second year when he passed from this sphere to the next. Shortly before he passed, while in the hospital, he prepared a message for all the members of his movement. It was simple and clear, so typical of him:

"Illness does not exist, delusion does not exist, sin does not exist. This is the fundamental truth of Seicho-No-Ie. God will now permit me to restfully sleep."

SEVEN

Years of Opportunity, Years of Unfoldment

Evidence of the dawning of a new era unfolded in the mid-1960's. Increasingly, indications that Dark Age influences were receding could be discerned. More and more, one could sense that something of major import was happening on the planet. Twenty years later would see the time-phase which many would refer to as "the hour of God," the point in history when a major shift in planetary consciousness would be recognized and humanity would begin to experience an increasing acceleration of spiritual awakening, an awakening which would reflect as an actualization of divine qualities in human affairs.

It was during this time, with the years of preparation behind me, that I was led to experience a more stable foundation for the unfoldment of the ministry. I use the word "unfoldment" because I have never attempted to *force* anything to happen relative to the work to which I have been called. I have always been keenly aware that the best plans devised by the mind of man, when working from the personality-sense, often come to purposeless ends. On the other hand, when one is open to inner guidance, unfoldments occur which have the signature of Providence upon them.

Settling in Florida, on Treasure Island west of St. Peters-

American INTA members at European congress, 1983; Dr. Blaine Mays, front center.

burg, I rented modest office space, accepted the help of a small staff of paid and volunteer workers, and entered into a program of lecturing, writing and publishing. Every year I visited dozens of cities to offer programs, speaking to ever larger groups of seekers, often as an invited guest at major New Thought churches and regional conferences. Emphasis upon seminars continued, so that more intensive work could be done with students, disciples, and persons interested in learning Kriya Yoga techniques.

Among the many thousands who attended my classes during those years, only a few hundred have remained true to their promised commitment to continue their involvement with spiritual practices. This is how it is with human nature; one may have the best of intentions but not continue on the chosen path because of the pressure of internal and external drives and influences. Paramahansa Yogananda observed similar student behavior during his years of consecrated work with presumed seekers on the path. One new on the path may truly be impassioned to "follow the path of right action" to spiritual freedom, only later to lose interest for one reason or another. The *way* is clear and direct, but how often we complicate the process; how easy it is to allow personal whims and fancies to blind us to the obvious!

I noticed, during those years, an increasing acceptance of Yoga philosophy and a growing interest among the population in learning how to meditate. At public lectures, after I had appeared on television or been interviewed by a newspaper reporter, many people who had not before attended such a program would come forward and tell me of their newly awakened interest.

In later years, on the other hand, I would ask during a program for a show of hands, to find out how many present were practicing meditation on a daily schedule, how many who formerly practiced no longer did so, and how many had never meditated until that program. The percentages were almost always similar: a few meditated daily, many who used to meditate had been neglecting their practices, and only a few had never meditated before.

Dedication of CSA Shrine of All Faiths and Sacred Initiation Temple, July, 1983

In my mind I would again hear my guru's voice: "Let your devotion to God be like a wood fire, which burns steadily and for a long time, and not like a straw fire which flashes up and then quickly goes out!"

While I feel compassion for those who have not remained steady on their chosen path, I do not let knowledge of this dampen my spirits, because I know that we are but in the early period of an enlightened era; it is human nature to waver, no matter how great the resolve at the outset. In the years to come, we will see millions of men and women living with total dedication to the highest ideals. As inertia is cleared from human consciousness, soul light will increasingly shine and mental and emotional confusion will dissolve.

Shortly after I had established a working base for the ministry in Florida, I began to see almost daily reports in the news media on the dramatic impact that Maharishi Mahesh Yogi was having upon the consciousness of people around the world. An intelligent and dedicated man, Maharishi encouraged the use of mantra as a meditation tool. His approach offered any reasonably conscious person an opportunity to experience the deep silence, and to enjoy the many benefits resulting from superconscious meditation. He referred to the process as Transcendental Meditation, because the ideal was to allow attention to flow with the mantra to the field of pure Being. There was nothing complicated about the process and it could be learned easily.

Public response to Maharishi varied. Some saw him merely as a nice little man who always seemed happy, and whose teaching was uncomplicated. Not a few were somewhat suspicious because his teaching was so simple and direct. And, naturally, many self-proclaimed spokespersons for the public good expressed their distrust of meditation. A few fundamentalist ministers expressed their concern that perhaps Maharishi was really interested in converting Americans to Hinduism.

None of this seemed to bother Maharishi, however. He continued his public work, and trained thousands of meditation teachers. Eventually, millions of people who had never meditated before were daily flowing into the silence, their attention flowing with their mantra. Of these millions who were attracted to the idea of meditation, many have since dropped away. Many meditators, however, have remained steady in their resolve, with benefit to themselves, and to the world.

Mantra meditation, correctly experienced, allows attention to be led from gross, to subtle, to fine perceptions of mind and consciousness. Eventually the meditator's attention transcends the mind and its modifications, and pure awareness is experienced. It is this experience of pure awareness which causes useful changes: the ordering of thought processes, reduction of stress, improved body function, refinement of the nervous system, clearing of the faculty of discernment, awakened intuition, and the awakening of dormant soul forces. Regular superconscious meditation "keeps the door open" between the superconscious field and the mind, so that superconscious influences continue to invade the mind to cleanse it of destructive drives and tendencies.

One useful result of the increased public awareness of meditation was that researchers at university levels began to be interested. They observed and tested volunteer meditators during meditation and gathered the results. It was found that when a person meditates correctly, certain physiological signs are present which are not evident during other known states of human consciousness. Breathing slows, heart action slows, brain wave patterns become synchronized, less oxygen is consumed by the body, less carbon dioxide is produced, and blood lactate levels drop, indicating stress reduction. These body responses are not found together during other known states of consciousness: not during ordinary sleep, not during the waking state, and not during hypnotic trance. All indications from the research are that meditation results in a state of relaxed conscious awareness which seems beneficial to both mind and body functions.

Armed with this data, many physicians began to recommend meditation to their patients as a tool to help them to reduce hypertension, lower high blood pressure, and even to regulate body processes which were formerly believed to be totally involuntary, beyond reach of one's conscious volition to regulate.

It has long been known, to some, that we can literally think ourselves into a condition of health, or into a condition of disease. When a person cultivates self-esteem, confidence, trust, and an appreciation for life, the body actually functions more efficiently. Internal secretions which strengthen the body's immune systems are produced by the brain and endocrine glands. On the other hand, when one allows himself to be a victim of low self-esteem, when one is fearful and anxious, when living seems to be a threat, body processes are inhibited and the immune systems are weakened. There is, after all, something to the statement, "Laughter is the best medicine!" To the person who is hurting, it may seem strange advice— to cultivate inner happiness, optimism, trust, and feelings of gratitude. Yet, this is precisely what should be done if one is to encourage inner processes to function correctly.

In counseling, I have often noted that, strange as it seems, some people seem to *prefer* limitations in their lives. A common statement is, "I don't like myself very much." Another is, "I'm afraid to make a decision, for fear I will make the wrong one." Then there are the rationalizations: "I've been told my condition is karmic," "My astrologer tells me that my problems are due to planetary influences," and so on. Now and then a person will ask, "How can I be sure that my illness (or problem of whatever nature) isn't God's will?"

One way to experience true self-esteem is to cultivate soul awareness and to enter into an intimate relationship with God. Deep meditation, the reading of inspirational literature, cultivating relationships which are mutually useful and supportive, and learning to accomplish worthy purposes—all these will contribute greatly to the enhancement of the realization of self-worth.

Decision-making takes practice. It is by actually making decisions that one has the opportunity to learn by experience how to make correct decisions. It is useful to think in terms of what is correct in any given situation, and not to be compelled by emotional drives.

Of course, what we now experience is the effect of prior causes. Our thoughts, expectations, desires, actions and states of consciousness determine our circumstances. Once we learn to discern the relationship between causes and effects, we can consciously choose how to think, how to anticipate, how to behave, and how to adjust our attitude so that orderly unfoldment is the rule for us. Present conditions can be changed by taking action in the present. Present conditions are not fixed in space and time because of past causes.

It is true that we are influenced by forces in our environment, not only in the immediate environment but also the larger environment of the world and the cosmos. Life is one organic whole, and no aspect of life is isolated. But to conclude that we are totally at the mercy of external influences is to say that we are mere victims of circumstance. The truth is that we are gods, and the more God-conscious we are, the more we discover that we flow through circumstances with the support of the uplifting current of the universe. As we remain open to the flow of superconscious forces, planetary consciousness is infused with them and, through us, the process of redemption continues, uplifting influences counteract darkening influences, and order is introduced into our world.

For some years I had been sending a regular newsletter to persons who attended my lectures and who requested literature; in 1967 I began the regular publication of a magazine, *Truth Journal*, which continues to grow in both circulation and influence today. A companion magazine, *CSA Magazin*, was started a few years later in Germany. *Truth Journal* carries articles written by myself and others, as well as ministry news and announcements of programs and publications.

Knowing the value of a regular study program, I have for years prepared monthly lessons which are mailed to those who request them: the *Studies in Truth* lesson series provides a theme each month, and practical suggestions for implementing the teachings.

Over the years, I have always had the good fortune to meet companion souls on the path, those who have a similar philosophical outlook and with whom an unspoken understanding is shared. Some such relationships are obviously due to proximity and shared ideals; at other times, it is as though a karmic link is present, a matter of shared destiny.

One such special person is Sri Swami Rama. We first met in 1969, in Detroit, Michigan, where both of us had been scheduled to speak during a weekend conference. Swamiji had just arrived in this country, and his maiden speech in America was given at that conference.

A handsome man of mercurial personality, Swami Rama quickly attracts attention even in a crowded arena. We visited briefly during the conference; later, after he had founded an Institute in a Chicago suburb, we had the opportunity to become more fully acquainted when I accepted an invitation to conduct a seminar there. It was then that I discovered that we had common spiritual roots; we both trace our lineage to the masters of the Himalayas. Trained from a very early age in the practice of Yoga by a Himalayan guru whose name I still do not know, Swamiji was also educated at schools and universities in India, Japan and Europe.

After coming to the United States, he lectured widely. He also allowed himself to be monitored at the famed Menninger Clinic in Topeka, Kansas, where he amazed the research team with his ability to consciously control autonomic functions of the body. Swamiji's role in that research project contributed greatly to further interest among scientists. His ability to actually demonstrate yogic claims has amazed and motivated many people since then. He once told me that the reason he actively engaged himself in demonstrating such abilities was in order to encourage the healing professions to utilize such processes in the treatment of their patients, and because his guru had instructed him to do this. His major interest, however, is in working with disciples who are sincerely devoted to inner transformation leading to Self-realization.

In 1975 Swami Rama, through the organization which he founded, the Himalayan International Institute of Yoga Science and Philosophy, sponsored the first annual Yoga Congress in Chicago. In later years, programs were convened in New York City and, finally, at the Institute's magnificent head-

Sri Swami Rama.

quarters, nestled amid rolling hills and forests near Honesdale, Pennsylvania. I have been a frequent guest teacher at the annual programs and have always enjoyed the friendship of many of the well-trained staff. Educated, principled, professional, Institute staff members are also disciples of Swamiji and dedicated to living the principles they teach. Among the services offered at the Institute are instruction in all of the Yoga systems, medical evaluation and treatment, psychological counseling, bio-feedback training, nutrition programs, and resident self-transformation opportunities. A publishing department makes available scores of books and periodicals, most of which are authored by Swami Rama, staff members, and leaders of the organization's branches in other cities.

I have just mentioned the value of "living the principles." This is a major problem for many; I have frequently observed that, among people who profess to be on the spiritual path, many are unwilling to assume personal responsibility for their actions. Even when they ask for, and receive, practical advice from a qualified person, such people will continue to dramatize immature roles. For example, on at least two occasions I have referred persons to the Himalayan Institute, after being asked to suggest a holistic center where help might be available to solve personal problems, only to have the persons in question later tell me "I contacted them, but they seemed too professional for my liking." They were really saying, "I contacted the office there and found out that I was going to have to be responsible in the therapy program, and I'm not ready to face that yet."

The inclination of many, who seem at first glance to be reasonably intelligent, to persist in useless involvements when they "know better" is also interesting to observe. For instance, I know of no enlightened person who endorses the practice of mediumship. Paramahansaji, before he made his transition, told some people, "Do not try to contact me through a medium after I am gone, because masters do not work through mediums." Yet, a few months after his passing, several nationally known "mediums" claimed to be in contact with my guru; some even wrote books about it!

Once, while on a speaking tour in the midwest, I met a woman who had a few years earlier attended my lectures in another city. She was, at that time, attending church services conducted by one of my brother disciples. I inquired how she was and what she was doing. She informed me that she was no longer attending my brother disciple's programs but was, instead, attending a weekly seance during which Paramahansaji "came through" and talked to the group. Since I thought I knew her quite well, I said, "It's not true, you know. Master said he would never speak through a medium. The person who is purporting to be in contact with him is either deluded or a liar." She looked me in the eye, smiled a self-satisfied smile and told me, "I know what you say may be true, because you knew Yoganandaji, but the lectures are so inspiring!"

It helps to be a yogi, one who is unmoved in the face of anything, at times like that.

Shortly after Swami Rama began his public work in America he was invited to speak at a conference in a western state. He found out that the sponsoring group strongly emphasized the usefulness of "channeling" messages from "masters" who supposedly resided in the subtle spheres. I will not repeat the whole story, but I can report that Swami Rama was not pleased with the situation, and he let it be known to everyone there. When I heard about the circumstances, I inwardly affirmed, "Bravo, Swamiji! Tell it like it is!"

I was born with discernment relative to matters concerning God and God's reality in, and as, the world. From my early years I have felt God's presence, and even when I did not know everything about God, I knew what was not so about God. I could always recognize untruth. I also always knew, from early on, that the better way was to pray, to spend time alone, to read the works of the masters, and to enjoy fellowship with saintly beings. That much I knew, even while the veils were lifting and increasing realizations were yet to be experienced.

One of the most perplexing challenges for many on the spiritual path is that of having the courage to say "no" when being enticed into a relationship or involvement which is inwardly intuited as nonuseful. We experience this while on the job, while relating with friends, and during the course of an average day as we make our rounds to attend to necessary duties. How and when to say "yes," and how and when to say "no" to offers that life presents is one of the more critical spiritual opportunities. Master sometimes referred to life's challenges as tests, similar to unannounced examinations one might be given while in high school or college. How well prepared we are, and how well we do on the tests, reveals much about our present capacities and state of consciousness.

God does not test us; life itself offers ample opportunity for us to see ourselves as we are at any given moment. Every time we "pass" we grow; every time we "fail" we also have an opportunity to grow, if we learn sufficiently from the experience—enough so that we will not fail again.

In 1970, in Dallas, Texas, I was speaking for Unity Church at the invitation of the minister, Dr. Donald Curtis. After one lecture, an Indian couple approached me and invited me to come to their nearby Yoga center for lunch the next day.

Upon entering the building I saw an impressive face looking back at me from the cover of a book on display. I asked my hosts, "Who is that man?" and was informed that he was Swami Muktananda, only recently arrived in the United States and then speaking in New York City. My hosts insisted that I accept Muktananda's book as a gift, and further informed me that he would be traveling throughout the country later that year. I made a mental note to meet him if the opportunity was convenient. As it turned out, it was more than convenient—it was already "arranged."

A few months later, I was speaking in California, and a disciple, Richard Rosager, had offered to drive me from Orange County to Los Angeles, where my next lecture was scheduled. Enroute he suggested we stop at a popular vegetarian restaurant for lunch. After enjoying a good meal, we proceeded down a hallway to the parking lot. I paused as I saw a large poster announcing a lecture by Swami Muktananda to be given the next evening, just a few blocks from the hotel where I was scheduled to stay.

Checking into the hotel, I invited Richard to my room to

Friends and disciples join me to visit Swami Muktananda at his ashram near Oakland, California, in 1976.

share a quiet interlude of meditation. Just as we were settling down to meditate, the telephone rang. It was Bob Raymer, a brother disciple. We talked for a few minutes, and I asked him, "Bob, you've been to India and you've met some of the yogis there. What do you know about a Swami Muktananda?"

Bob laughed and said, "He's my house guest."

I told him that I knew of the lecture the following evening and that I would see him there. Richard and I then meditated for a while, and I later prepared for my talk that evening.

The audience was receptive that evening and, at the close of my talk, during which I announced the Saturday meditation seminar two days hence, I also announced, "Tomorrow evening is open. I've heard of a lecture which I plan to attend. It's by Swami Muktananda. I haven't met him but I've seen his picture and I know he's a strong yogi. Why don't you join me there?" I gave further specifics about time and location and then mingled with the people.

A young man with sparkling eyes came up to me and said, "I'm Franklin Jones. Muktananda is my guru. I'll be glad to introduce you to him." We agreed to meet the next afternoon at Bob Raymer's house in Pacific Palisades.

That night, during a vivid dream, I met Swami Muktananda. I had read in his book some references to the "blue pearl" which is perceived by meditators when prana flows to the spiritual eye and crown chakra. I felt that he must have been writing about the spiritual eye as I knew it, because of the various descriptions he provided from his own experiences. In my dream, Muktananda spoke fluent English. I asked him, "What do you mean by the term 'blue pearl'?" He smiled and said, "You know, the spiritual eye."

Richard drove me to Bob's house and we arrived on schedule. We were invited into a large living room where several others had already gathered and were sitting quietly. I greeted several, because they had sometimes attended my lectures. Muktananda, I was informed, was just about to come from a nearby room, where he had been resting.

When he joined us he was wearing a rumpled ochre shirt and *dhoti*. Striding about barefoot, his wide smile welcoming us, his unspoken statement was, "You are my guests. You have honored me. Please be comfortable." After pausing briefly to talk quietly with two or three people, he settled down on a large couch around which everyone else had gathered, sitting on the floor.

I was introduced to him and, through an interpreter, we discussed a few matters of mutual interest. He knew of Mahavatar Babaji, he said, but had met him only through inner vision. Then, to verify the dream experience of the previous night, I asked him, "What do you mean by the 'blue pearl'?" He said, "You know. Your guru speaks of it in his autobiography. It's the same thing."

Muktananda was well received in America; eventually he established two large ashrams, one near Oakland, California, and the other in New York State, about an hour's drive from Manhattan. Over the years, when our travel schedules coincided, I would visit him at one of his gatherings, sometimes taking along a few friends. He was always the perfect host, gracious and attentive. Once, after he had concluded a retreat in a mountain setting about ten miles north of CSA Lakemont, I invited him to visit our center, which he did. He was shown through the printing plant, given a tour of the grounds and, with a few of his disciples, served light refreshments.

Shaktipat, the transmission of spiritual force, was emphasized at Muktananda's programs. With those close to him he was a strict disciplinarian, but he was just as strict with himself. He would awaken before dawn to meditate, and then be intensely involved with supervising activities, seeing visitors, and handling various organizational matters.

On one of his visits to America he was sponsored in San Francisco, Los Angeles, and New York City by Werner Erhard's *est* Foundation. I attended the opening program in San Francisco, where well over two thousand people gathered. Werner introduced Muktananda, who came onto the stage to sustained applause and talked for an hour or so. I thought his message that evening was superficial, and I noticed that many in the audience, for whom this was the first introduction to a yogi, seemed not to understand even the obvious points he made.

The following morning, I was sitting with him and his interpreter while visitors came and went. During an interlude, Muktananda said, "Last night was for the public. Tonight, I'll say what I want to say!"

It was a rainy morning in Nuremberg, Germany, October 31, 1982, when I awakened from sleep after dreaming of Swami Muktananda. I had lectured the night before and was scheduled to drive to Munich later that day. While having breakfast I read the European edition of the Herald Tribune, and on one of the back pages I saw a small news item: Muktananda had made his transition the day before, at his ashram in Ganeshpuri, north of Bombay. He was 72 years of age, a warrior spirit to the last. Before he passed he had chosen to succeed him two young disciples, brother and sister, who had been close to him from their early childhood. The brother stepped down three years later, leaving his sister, Swami Chidvilasananda, as the guru in Muktananda's *siddha* tradition.

It is seldom that gurus from India teach with exactly the same emphasis when they visit the West. Swami Vivekananda, disciple of Sri Ramakrishna, brought the message of Vedanta at the turn of the century. Paramahansa Yogananda made yogic procedures acceptable to hundreds of thousands because of his practical approach, and his emphasis upon Kriya Yoga meditation techniques as a certain way to God-realization. Maharishi Mahesh Yogi was also able, because of his practical, scientific emphasis, to reach people who before had either not known about or not been inclined to become involved in meditation practice. Swami Rama, Swami Muktananda, and others have made their unique contributions because of their destined missions.

It would be a mistake for Europeans and Americans to emotionally adopt an Eastern lifestyle, thinking this to be important to their spiritual progress. The great essential is to accept what is useful, what is workable, and include it in one's personal life. Even the New Thought movement of today, whose adherents frequently assert has its origins in America, tells but part of the story. What is now known as New Thought is but a fragment of a larger body of philosophical knowledge known as *Sanatana Dharma*, "the eternal way of righteousness," which has roots in the Middle East and India. Early New Thought pioneers, Charles Fillmore and Ernest Holmes among them, knew this and would often speak of it in private circles.

Mary Baker Eddy's "revelation" of Christian Science was merely a simple restatement of absolute monism: one Thing exists and is responsible for all outer appearances. It is believed by many that Mrs. Eddy knew this, but chose to proclaim the teaching as her own original discovery because of the impact it would have on the public.

Thomas Troward, whose books on Mental Science were widely used as class texts by early New Thought teachers, learned about the principles of which he wrote in India, while he was in that country serving as a judge. Thousands of people who today attend various New Thought churches and centers still have not heard of, much less read the *Bhagavad Gita* or the *Yoga Sutras*, which, in their terse verses offer a comprehensive explanation of everything New Thought stands for—and more.

I am occasionally asked if I discern any increase in the numbers of people indicating an interest in Self-actualization. Of course, millions of people today are looking for answers to pressing problems, and seeking to know more about the nature of consciousness. However, along with the increase in numbers, I can also observe increasing evidence of confusion among the ranks of seekers.

One reason for this is that many who are sincerely interested in spiritual matters are also sadly lacking in discernment. They often conclude that anything new must be useful to know about, and that anything glamorous must be examined. Man is curious, and in his efforts to satisfy his curiosity he often learns many useful things, but when one is lacking in powers of discernment, curiosity can lead one into a variety of complicated circumstances. Many spend years "shopping" in the "spiritual supermarket" without ever really settling down to one working program which could result in inner transformation and Self-realization, if only they would follow it.

For one on the spiritual path, regardless of the tradition to which he belongs, the proven way to fulfillment is *repentance, commitment* and *process.* Once the possibility of soul freedom is glimpsed, then commitment on the path and intentional involvement with principles and procedures can alone guarantee success. Whether one identifies with Christianity, Hinduism, Buddhism, Judaism, or any other valid tradition, the basic approach to God remains the same.

Through many years of ministry service I have witnessed dramatic healings and marvelous evidence of positive change in the lives of many hundreds of people. I have seen response that far exceeds my personal efforts to share truth principles. I know at such times that the goodness of God is the operant influence, and I am thankful.

EIGHT

To India,
as a Pilgrim

When I first went to India I did not go to seek a teacher or to discover anything new. I went as an act of devotion. I wanted to see and experience that land known as the mother of religions. I lived there once, during a previous embodiment, and I was somewhat curious about how it would feel to be there again.

During the spring of 1972 I was in southern California and had been invited to be one of three panelists on a radio talk show. One of the others invited was Russian-born Indra Devi, then a popular author of books on Hatha Yoga. Towards the end of the one-hour broadcast, our host asked each member of the panel to share closing remarks. Indra Devi began talking about a holy man in India who could perform genuine miracles. I later talked with her privately and she told me more about Sri Satya Sai Baba.

A few months later, while I was talking with a radio producer in Orlando, Florida, the subject of India came up. I mentioned Sai Baba's name and the producer reached into a desk drawer and took out a book about him. Handing it to me, he said, "My good friend, Indra Devi, gave this to me. Take it with you and let me know what you think about it."

The contents of that book were interesting. The author, Mr. Kasturi, told of Satya Sai Baba's early years, of his miracle-working abilities, of his charisma, and of the fact that millions in India consider him to be an avatar, a full manifestation of Divine Power. Born in a small village in South India, Sai Baba began to attract attention at an early age because of his ability to know things about people, to prescribe procedures to cure ailments and, most of all, because he had the ability to "pull out of the air" with a movement of his hand anything he willed. Prayer beads, amulets, rings adorned with sacred imagery, medicine, candy, flowers—anything he willed would instantly materialize in his hand.

His parents, thinking him to be possessed, took him to a series of exorcists. But he was not possessed; he had simply been born with the ability to do unusual things. At the age of fourteen he left home to live with a relative. He dropped out of school at that time and became available to people in need of advice and help of various kinds. He also conducted weekly devotional meetings. As the years passed, his fame spread throughout India and pilgrims began to come to him in increasing numbers.

Satya Sai Baba claims that he is the reincarnation of Sai Baba of Shirdi, an eccentric saint who departed the world eight years before Satya Sai Baba was born. He further says that he will remain in his present body until the year A.D. 2021, when he will be ninety-five years of age. He will then be reborn in South India and be known as Prema Sai Baba.

On my next visit to California I met Walter and Elsie Cowan, who were devotees of Satya Sai Baba. Walter and Elsie appeared to be in their early seventies. They were very generous with their time and information about their experiences with Sai Baba, and while we were talking Elsie suddenly said to me, "We'll be going to India in October. Why don't you go along with us?" I explained that my own travel plans for the remainder of the year were not yet firm, but that I would keep her offer in mind.

In October I conducted a weekend seminar in New York.

Sri Satya Sai Baba, world teacher.

At the conclusion of the seminar, since I had a passport and some free time, out of curiosity I went to an Air India ticket office and inquired about schedules and prices for a roundtrip flight between New York and Bombay. I was told that I could be booked on a flight that evening, and the price was modest. On an impulse, I purchased the tickets, went to the Indian Embassy to apply for a visa, and a few hours later was enroute to Bombay.

Twenty-two hours later, after stops in several cities along the way, we landed at Bombay. It was just after dawn. Because of a delay we had experienced at the Rome airport, where the baggage handlers had gone on a one-hour strike, I missed my connection to Bangalore, my final destination. An airline representative in Bombay provided me with a card which I was to present at the desk of the Taj Mahal Hotel, providing me with a room until the next available flight to Bangalore.

The hotel was modern and comfortable. After a few hours of rest I went down to the lobby to arrange for a taxi back to the airport. Across the lobby I saw a woman, her back to me, talking with the bell captain. She looked familiar, and I approached to verify that, indeed, she was Elsie Cowan. Our reunion was a joyful one and could not have been more perfectly timed had we arranged it, although I had not known her travel schedule and she had not known even whether I would be traveling to India or not.

Arriving in Bangalore after dark, I went to the West End Hotel and checked in. This facility was an older one, with low buildings and extensive gardens. At that time, it was one of the more popular hotels for Sai Baba devotees to use while in Bangalore. It was comfortable, the service was good, and prices were modest.

The next morning after breakfast, I walked around the grounds until about ten, then decided to hire a taxi to take me to Whitefield, some fifteen miles from Bangalore, where I had heard Sai Baba had a residence and where a school for boys was being developed. When we arrived at the Whitefield compound, a group of one hundred or more people were sitting under a banyon tree on the grounds, chanting softly. Satya

With Professor V.K. Gokak, at the Rome conference, October, 1983.

Sai Baba walked slowly about the grounds, stopping now and then to wave his hand and produce something for a devotee, or just to share a few words. After a while, he went into his house, and I asked the taxi driver to take me back to the hotel.

In the hotel restaurant I was greeted by Walter and Elsie, Indra Devi, and a few others who were there. Elsie said, "We told Baba about you; he wants you to come with us tonight at six o'clock, when we are invited to see him."

My first encounter with Sai Baba was pleasant. I sat, with a group of about two dozen people, on the floor in the front room of the main house at Whitefield. Sai Baba came into the room, smiled and greeted everyone, and then sat down with us. It was a pleasant hour or so of interchange, as he talked, asked questions, answered questions, and made everyone feel good. At one point he turned to me and said, "You know, it is not enough merely to be the disciple of a great guru. One must become like the guru."

The next day, about a dozen of us were invited to spend almost the whole day at Sai Baba's house, sometimes talking with him, sometimes just being there while he went out to see people gathered on the grounds in front of the residence. In the afternoon I sat with Walter and Elsie as they asked Sai Baba's advice on procedures connected with the center they had started in Orange County, California. They had a long list of questions; I read the questions and Sai Baba gave the answers. After a while he called Professor Gokak over to join us and said, "Here, you talk with Gokak. Whatever he can't answer I'll answer when I get back." With that he walked out.

In about an hour he returned. Almost all of the questions had been answered. The final one was for permission to edit and publish in America a small book that had formerly been available only in India. It was a collection of sayings of Sai Baba. He readily gave his permission, and I was assigned the responsibility for editing and publishing the book. A few months later, it was published by CSA Press as *The Teachings of Sri Satya Sai Baba.*

On the third day of our visit, a caravan of cars followed

Sai Baba's car as it wended its way through the countryside from Bangalore to Prasanti Nilayam, "the Abode of Peace," Sai Baba's chief ashram near Puttaparthi. The journey of approximately one hundred miles took about four hours to complete because the road was narrow and went through several villages, where it was often blocked by cows, goats, and human activity of various kinds. As Sai Baba's car passed fields in which men were working, they would raise their arms and shout, "Sri Satya Sai Babaji, Ji!"

I was assigned a room in a cottage near the main entrance gate of the ashram. Two other men shared the cottage with me. For the next ten days I gathered, with others, for morning and afternoon *darshan*, the occasion when Sai Baba would walk among the people, talking with them and blessing them with his presence. From time to time he would choose individuals or groups for private interviews and send them to the porch of the temple to await his arrival a few minutes later.

Because I was with Walter and Elsie I was invited to sit with them whenever they attended group interview sessions. Even when the Cowans returned to Bangalore for a few days, Sai Baba continued to motion for me to join interview groups. In this way I was able on several occasions to observe him closely as he worked with the people.

Group interview sessions were informal. People would sit on the floor facing Sai Baba. He would encourage discussion and talk for a while with one person and then another. Always, when a session would end, Sai Baba would ask the people to stand while he walked from person to person for a final word with them. And always, before he turned to the next person, he would move his hand in a circular motion and produce a token of his grace—a ring, a necklace, or a small quantity of sacred ash, which he would usually request the person to place on the tongue and consume for its medicinal qualities.

One afternoon, only a few Americans were in the interview room with Sai Baba. I sat to his left, our knees almost touching. Looking at a man directly in front of him, Sai Baba raised his open hand and said, "Look!" Then he closed his hand and held it at knee level. In a moment we could see his hand opening, forced by something which was emerging from his palm. A moment later he held in his hand a large mass of candy. Breaking it into small chunks, he passed it around to be shared by the group. A small towel lay on the floor beside Sai Baba; I handed it to him so that he could wipe the crumbs from his hand, and he did so. Then, turning to me, he slapped my knee and said, "Everything is one thing. Do you agree?"

Satya Sai Baba has the ability to bring together subtle element-influences to form any substance he desires. He does it as easily as the average person might perform a routine task. There is no effort on his part, only intention and will, and the object is produced. During one of the group sessions, someone asked him, "How do you do it?" He chuckled and said, "I have self-confidence."

On another occasion a young man from Madras handed Sai Baba a handwritten letter. The man's wife was in a hospital and the diagnosis was cancer. Sai Baba quickly read the letter, looked at the enclosed snapshot of the woman, reflected a moment, then turned to the man and said, "I'll take care of it." When Sai Baba says that, the healing process begins immediately, even if the patient is hundreds or thousands of miles distant.

At the conclusion of that group session, Sai Baba went to each person in the room and produced something for him or her. When he came to the young man, who was standing with his hands out waiting for Sai Baba to materialize something for him, he slapped him affectionately on the shoulder and said, "I've already given you back your wife." Then he turned to me and asked, "When are you leaving?" I had been thinking of leaving the following afternoon but had not discussed it with him. When I informed him of my plans, he said, "See me at eight o'clock tomorrow morning, right here."

Late that evening I walked the ashram grounds. I knew that the next morning, during our private time together, Sai Baba would ask me what I would like to have from him. I had no philosophical questions, and no personal problems. I planned merely to thank him for his hospitality. I knew that he would materialize something for me as a keepsake, and that he would ask me to choose what he should produce. Not wanting to be without an answer, I thought, "Well, if he asks me that, I'll say that a simple ruby ring will be fine." I was thinking of a star ruby, a common stone for the purpose.

The next morning I was invited into the interview room along with a small group of Indian men. One by one Sai Baba took the men into a corner of the room and held a whispered conversation. Then he waved for me to join him. Without asking me anything, he began to tell me about myself and about some people with whom I was involved, assuring me that I was doing good work and that everything would continue to unfold. Then, looking at me, he asked, "What can I give you?" I responded, "Nothing, sir, just your blessing."

With that he placed his hand on my chest and began to rub it with a firm circular motion, meanwhile saying, "You already have that. What can I give you as a keepsake?"

I answered, "Anything you like, sir, but it's not really necessary."

Before the sentence was finished he stepped back, moved his hand in a circle, closed his fist to catch whatever had been materialized, and placed in my hand a ruby ring, saying, "Here, a gold ring with my picture."

The ring, which I still have today, is intricately designed with an enamel portrait of Sai Baba set in gold. The portrait is surrounded by twenty-two small faceted rubies. When I put it on, it fit my ring finger perfectly.

Sai Baba says that he gives such talismans as a point of contact between him and the person to whom it is given. In this way a connection is made, so that wherever in the world the person may be, Sai Baba maintains a telepathic rapport with the person.

Nine years later, in 1981, I returned to India, this time going first to New Delhi, then to Ranchi to visit the boys' school which Paramahansaji had founded in 1917, then on to Bangalore and Prasanti Nilayam. At Ranchi I was given a tour of the facility by the resident swami, an American, and shown the small room where Master slept and meditated during the early days of the school, before he went to America. The room is maintained as a shrine and a place of pilgrimage for devotees of my guru line. I had planned to go on to visit the Yogoda Satsanga headquarters at Dakshineshwar, Calcutta, but plans were changed at the last moment.

Flying back to New Delhi from Ranchi, the plane made a stop at Benares, and I was able to enjoy a good view of the city and the Ganges River from where I sat.

When I arrived in Bangalore I checked into a convenient hotel and rested for a few days, sometimes walking about parts of the city and at other times remaining in my room to read. I placed a telephone call to Professor Gokak and informed him that I would be arriving at Prasanti Nilayam the next day.

I had been in correspondence with Professor Gokak, because a party of thirty people, a few from North America but most of them from Europe, planned to meet me at the ashram in time to attend Sai Baba's birthday celebration. Our group was given quarters in one of the newly built hotels on the ashram grounds, sleeping several men or women to a room. At least one hundred thousand people were expected for the celebration. Room accommodations could not satisfy the demand, and the majority who would attend would have to sleep in large covered sheds, using their own bedding brought from home.

Because of the large numbers of people gathered, and because Sai Baba was busy with the heads of his organization, I did not talk with him during that visit, although I did attend all of the darshan sessions and many of the public meetings. Baba seemed more cosmic than ever, and still moved with grace and assurance. A major event during that celebration week was the occasion when representatives of the Indian government arrived at the ashram to attend a mass meeting and officially declare Sai Baba's educational system as having official university status in India.

For years the Sai Baba organization had been active, building colleges in many states of India. What is unique about Sai Baba's colleges is that emphasis is placed upon service to man. The students must work to qualify for entrance into the colleges, and they must participate fully in all programs. They gather daily for devotional chanting and meditation and are taught the basic unity of all religions. They also work for a set number of hours every week in their communities, helping the underprivileged to improve the quality of their lives.

Sai Baba serves as Chancellor of the University and Professor Gokak was installed as Vice-Chancellor, in which capacity he served until November of 1985. Professor Gokak was in his early seventies when he accepted the position. A soft-spoken man, he is known throughout India as a scholar, author, poet and educator. When we first met, in 1972, we immediately established a warm and intimate relationship.

One of his books, which had been published in English in Bombay, interested me very much, and during the second India visit I asked him for permission to publish the book through CSA Press. He was pleased at my willingness to do this and readily granted permission. The book, *Narahari: Prophet of New India*, is written in the form of a novel, with the central character, Narahari, portrayed as a hero-figure with a world vision for the betterment of humanity. As the story unfolds one becomes aware that Narahari embodies the idealism and the personality characteristics of both Satya Sai Baba and Sri Aurobindo. Professor Gokak was a keen student of Sri Aurobindo for many years before he met Sai Baba. When he first met Sai Baba he experienced inner conflict, wondering whether he was being unfaithful to Sri Aurobindo because of his attraction to Sai Baba and his work. Sai Baba put his mind at ease on the matter.

Sri Aurobindo, who made his transition many years ago, is considered a philosopher-seer whose impact on planetary consciousness will long endure. Among other things, he emphasized the ideal of the descent of superconscious influences into the world through the enlightened consciousness of individuals. Although he lived for many years in seclusion, he worked always for the uplift of humanity. His vision of possibilities for mankind and Planet Earth was extraordinary, and because of it he was one of the special prophets of our time.

Someone once expressed the opinion that Sri Aurobindo's writings were "so intellectual that even most intellectuals can't understand them." Nevertheless, the force of his vision has inspired millions in a positive direction. In his early years, he was strongly in favor of political independence for India, and so vocal that he was imprisoned by the British, who at that time governed the country. It was while he was in prison that Aurobindo experienced inner transformation and was led of the Spirit to work for world good in a higher way.

It was a happy occasion for me to again be with Professor Gokak when the Satya Sai organization invited me to speak at an international symposium in Rome, at the end of October, 1983. Delegates from many countries were present, over three thousand strong. I spoke on the theme, *Spiritual Responsibilities in Our Fast-Awakening World: Our Duties and Great Opportunities.* A portion of my speech follows:

> What those who yet think in materialistic terms do not know is that there is currently a powerful evolutionary movement which is being felt throughout creation, and this movement is nothing less than the urge of God to fulfill His purposes. Some see this activity of God in the world as Divine intervention, and I feel that this is so. Built into the very fabric of nature is the urge in the direction of completion or fulfillment of purpose. Even when man strays from the intended purpose and goal of life, something moves within him and around him to put him on the right track again.
>
> Creation was not a divine accident. The whole process is being nourished, sustained and directed by God. But we must also do our part, because it is partly through us that God is able to manifest Himself and fulfill His purposes.
>
> The more open we are to God's influence, to His grace, the more willing we are to live in harmony with the laws of nature and to cultivate the virtues, the more responsive we are to do what can be done to meet human needs from a spiritual viewpoint, in practical ways, and to see hurts and heal them, the more God's influence can express.
>
> Every human being possesses a Buddha nature, the nature of enlightenment, the nature of true knowledge.

Addressing delegates at the international symposium in
Rome, October, 1983.

When the mind is purified, when the soul is awakened, the true nature shines brilliantly of its own accord. It seems that, more and more, the veil between the inner and the outer realms is becoming finer, more subtle, and the energies from the finer realms are becoming increasingly influential in the affairs of men. Each person here at this symposium is an important part of the grand evolutionary transformation now being experienced by mankind.

There are thousands of saints in the world. There are millions of good people who are doing their best to live responsible lives. There are also millions of confused people, disturbed people, and even some people whose efforts are destructive. This is all part of the human condition, but the human condition will improve over the next few decades as an increasing number of people become more conscious.

My pilgrimage to India was useful in many ways. Many new friendships were established and a better understanding of people and their aspirations and needs was acquired. Useful contacts were made with publishers and heads of ashrams. One result of the latter is that now more of our literature is being made available in India and a cooperative working relationship with leaders of groups is taking place.

During my first visit to India in 1972, while in Bombay prior to returning to America, out of curiosity I made an appointment with an astrologer. He was reputed to be one of several custodians of manuscripts, written centuries ago, by a group of astrologers working under the common name of Bhrigu. The popular belief is that before the beginning of the last Dark Age, astrologer-sages wrote in manuscripts the horoscopes of millions of people yet unborn, and circulated portions of the collection to various families who were to preserve them.

At any rate, I telephoned for an appointment and went to the address given. When I arrived I was greeted cordially and taken outdoors, where I was asked to stand with my back to the sun. The astrologer measured the length of my shadow, from the instep of my foot to where the shadow ended on the ground. We then went back into his apartment, and he began to pour through stacks of old papers. In this tradition, the astrologer is really more a reader of what has already been written in the manuscripts, and he does not really cast a horoscope. Instead, by calculating the time of day of the client's arrival for the reading, by measuring the angle of the sun, he is able to find the right reference material.

The Bhrigu reader asked me not to reveal any information about myself until after he had read from the manuscript. At first, he fumbled a little, made a few false starts, selected a different page from the stack in front of him, and began to read. Most of what he said was general, not specific. Finally, he correctly told me how many brothers and sisters I had, and whether they were younger or older than I. Then he said something very specific, especially interesting since I had told him nothing and was attired in ordinary western dress and displayed nothing that might indicate that I was a yogi. He said, "You began your studies in Yoga when you were twelve, and you attained proficiency when you were twenty-one years of age." It was true. I had become intensely involved in study at about the age he mentioned, and I was ordained by Paramahansaji during my twenty-first year.

When the reading was over we enjoyed a pleasant discussion about Paramahansaji, whom he knew about, and other matters of mutual interest. I have no idea whether he actually read from the manuscript, as he seemed to do, or whether he was using it as the presumed authority, while really doing an intuitive reading. The incident was not the most important one during my first India visit, but it was interesting. As I was preparing to leave, he looked once more into his records and said, "You will return to India in nine years." That statement would turn out to be true.

NINE

Everything is Given of God

Any worthwhile unfoldment must be attributed to grace. We can prepare ourselves, we can do the work before us, we can dream, we can meditate, we can pray. Whatever we do is our duty and our part in the process. Worthwhile unfoldments, those which truly bless us and others, are due to God's grace. Of this I am convinced.

This ministry has always been one of growth as the result of needs being met, often in unplanned ways. I cannot report all of the times when, in years past, I have experienced grace. I have seen doors open, miracles happen, and people touched and blessed in many ways as the result of grace.

In 1967, while giving a series of lectures in a hotel in downtown Atlanta, Georgia, I met Ed and Lois O'Neal. They had driven down from Lakemont, in the northeast Georgia mountains, to attend to business matters and had arranged their schedule so they could attend a lecture. Introducing themselves, they invited me to have dinner with them at a Chinese restaurant just across the street from the hotel. I remember well that during the time of those lectures in Atlanta, much of the South was experiencing the tension which resulted from civil rights activities, activities which were to bring about long overdue changes for millions of American citizens.

Ed and Lois informed me that they had, a few years earlier, founded a spiritual community at Lakemont and that one of the projects in which they were involved was the publishing of metaphysical books and literature. We shared information of mutual interest and they asked me for permission to publish one of my books, which had been out of print for a while. That was the beginning of our friendship, and of a relationship that would continue to mature.

The O'Neals, along with friends, founded Christian Spiritual Alliance, Inc., as a non-profit religious brotherhood in 1964. They had purchased a ten-acre site just off Lake Rabun Road, in Lakemont. The property was undeveloped, in a natural setting, with one building which they used as a residence. Their ideal was to establish a community, where people of any religious or philosophical persuasion could come to find support and encouragement. To help fund the project they had started, with borrowed money, a printing and publishing business which then occupied a small building about one mile down the road from the property. Before long, a rustic lodge was acquired, overlooking Lake Rabun. Here seminars were offered at various times during the year.

I continued to live in Florida, and maintained a regular schedule of lectures and classes in major cities of the country. I would also travel frequently to smaller communities, going wherever led. Each summer, I visited Lakemont to offer summer programs. In time, CSA Press, the publishing department, became the permanent publisher and distributor of all my books.

In 1971, while I was in residence at Lakemont for a summer program, the trustees invited me to become a lifetime board member and to assume responsibility for the spiritual leadership of CSA. It was an ideal relationship for everyone— I was then involved with an expanding ministry, but with no established base of operations. CSA had the physical plant and equipment, but needed spiritual leadership. After some discussion, it was agreed that I would join forces with them.

Feeling that the corporate name, Christian Spiritual Alliance, might not project a sufficiently broad image for an international ministry, I suggested that the teaching department be named Center for Spiritual Awareness. All office procedures were transferred to the newly built printing plant at Lakemont and a secretary was hired to process the mail and handle routine details. I remained in close contact with CSA through weekly reports, written memos, telephone conversations, and timely personal visits. The work grew rapidly during those cooperative years, and in 1973 I changed my residence from Florida to Lakemont.

Northeast Georgia is remarkable for its low mountain beauty and superb climate. During the summer months, thousands of tourists travel through Rabun County to enjoy the lush forested mountains, the sparkling lakes and the clear air. Autumn, when the leaves turn from green to rich browns, golds and reds, is spectacular. Winters are usually mild, with only occasional snow. The Cherokee Indians used to roam this area, which they considered sacred; it is still considered sacred by many in the area today.

Five miles distant is Tallulah Falls, Georgia, boasting the largest canyon this side of the Mississippi River. Just a few miles north, on Route 441, is Rabun Gap-Nacoochee School, now famous because of the bestselling Foxfire book series.

I am often asked why I chose Lakemont, Georgia, as the site of CSA. Well, I didn't choose it; it chose me! In prior years when visiting Georgia, I had always flown into Atlanta, and then traveled south to Florida. I had been thinking of a place for a retreat facility before meeting Ed and Lois, but north Georgia had never entered my mind as a possibility. It is ideal for the purpose. As the only retreat facility in the South offering regular programs in Yoga, stress management, nutrition and related themes, CSA is but a two-hour drive from Atlanta and accessible to persons who want to visit frequently from Florida, Alabama, Tennessee, North Carolina and South Carolina. Most who come here from a great distance fly into the Hartsfield Airport near Atlanta and rent a car or use public bus service, which is daily from Atlanta to Tallulah Falls. CSA provides transportation from Tallulah Falls for visitors.

CSA Meditation Hall, where retreat sessions are held.

CSA Shrine of All Faiths and Sacred Initiation Temple.
The library can be seen in the background.

An informal moment following a Kriya Yoga ceremony
at Lakemont.

Lois O'Neal made her transition on March 11, 1976, after a brief illness. She had been a strong and caring person and made possible much of the physical foundation upon which CSA Lakemont has grown. Before she passed, there had been some discussion about building a permanent teaching facility on the property and Lois had, in fact, marked off the area where the building was to be constructed. After her passing it was decided to go forward with the building project. A letter was sent to members and friends, a contractor was hired, and fourteen months after her passing the Lois B. O'Neal Memorial Meditation Hall was dedicated during the initial summer program of 1977; a bronze tablet was affixed to the outside front wall of the building.

The Meditation Hall is spacious and comfortable, ideal for the purposes for which it was conceived. Temperature-controlled, the main room is used for lectures and classes, as well as for our regular Sunday morning service. The room adjacent to the main hall serves as the dining area, where vegetarian meals are served during seminars and programs. Facilities for audio and video recording are also located in the building.

On October 22, 1977, Ed O'Neal decided to retire from CSA activities to pursue other interests, and I was named president of the board of trustees. As the spiritual director of CSA I am responsible for all matters relating to the ministry; members of the board of trustees give their support and participate in planning and decision-making to ensure the general welfare of the organization. Each trustee is a devotee on the path and a Kriya Yoga initiate.

CSA is not a spiritual community in the usually understood sense, and it is not a commune. It is a ministry whose headquarters at Lakemont is a service center, to which people come for spiritual refreshment and from which literature and other learning aids are sent around the world. The only permanent residents, besides myself, are a few of the paid staff members who prefer to live here. During the average year, hundreds of people visit for private and for public retreats, and several people who are attuned to the teaching emphasis live and work in Rabun County and attend programs at Lakemont. Spiritual communities and ashrams with permanent residents have value of course, but this is not our theme. The CSA ideal is for devotees of God to remain in society and live a pure life, while attending to duties and obligations. In this way society is infused with a special influence which is introduced into it through such conscious people.

There are some people whose nature it is, whose duty it is to live in relative seclusion in order to engage in research or to be involved with creative projects. It is useful for people in society to remove themselves, from time to time, from the pressures of social interaction for a duration of rest and inner refreshment. But the ideal for most people in today's world is to live a responsible life in the mainstream of society, while reserving private time daily for prayer and meditation and, always, being inwardly settled in understanding.

An ancient Middle East proverb states, "The ideal is to be able to buy and sell in the market place, and never lose sight of God." If this cannot be done, if it is not possible to live in the world, enjoying relationships and creative activities, and to do this with God-consciousness, then multiplied millions of men and women are doomed to failure on the spiritual path, no matter how strong their resolve. Where one lives and what one does is not as important as what one *is*, in consciousness. This is the determining factor; when one is inwardly attuned to God and His will, then all outer relationships and activities will be perfectly coordinated.

There once lived, in ancient India, a king named Janaka. He was also renowned as a great sage. One day, a disciple asked his guru, "I have heard of a great sage who is also a king. How can this be so? How can a person fulfill his worldly responsibilities and still be a sage?"

The guru replied, "Oh, you had better ask him. I know him and I will give you a letter of introduction. You go to him and ask him for yourself."

The disciple went to Janaka's palace and presented the letter of introduction. He also asked the question that he had earlier asked his guru. King Janaka said, "Here, put this pot filled with water on your head. Then walk about the palace grounds and return to me without spilling a drop. If you fail, I will have you punished."

The young man did as he was instructed, being very careful not to spill any water. When he returned, the king said, "Well done! Now, tell me what you saw during your little walk."

The disciple answered, "I saw nothing, great sir. My attention was totally directed to the water pot, as I dared not spill any water."

Then the king instructed, "Walk around the palace grounds again. Do not spill a drop of water but, this time, you must observe carefully everything that comes within range of your vision."

Much later, the seeker of truth returned, the water pot still filled. "Now," said the king, "Tell me what you saw!" The young man was able to relate all of his visual perceptions to the satisfaction of the king. Then, Janaka explained:

"Just as you were able to observe everything, without taking your attention from the water pot on your head, so I am able to move through this world without forgetting God."

One of the major challenges, for many people, is that of coming to terms with the material world. The material world is but an outer manifestation of Spirit. The problem faced by many is not the world itself, but their relationships in it, and their own attachments and aversions. This is why, when we are inwardly aware, when we clearly comprehend who we are and what the nature of the world really is, we are able to live in this, or any world, without problems. Liberation of consciousness does not mean separation from relationships; it means that one is inwardly free of concepts and conflicts which cause problems in relationships. It is attachment to relationships and things, or an inability to experience relationships and relate to things in a responsible way, which presents the major challenge to many.

The growth of the ministry has always followed needs. We have never promoted growth or worked to increase membership, except by offering services to meet needs. A person once wrote to me and confessed, "I liked CSA much better before you got so busy. I miss being able to correspond with you every week." And, of course, when we send occasional letters to our membership inviting their financial support, a few will let me know that it's not really "spiritual" to talk about money. I prefer to talk about God, and about the spiritual process, but a ministry requires financial fuel, energy which is converted into salaries, taxes, utilities payments, office costs, printing, postage, and all of the essentials relating to communicating the word and providing facilities. For people who work and who are compensated with a paycheck, money represents their time and energy given in exchange for that paycheck. Hopefully, the work they do is also a real service to society. Therefore, when one who earns money gives it to a worthy cause, he is giving a portion of his time and energy in the form of money, which is merely a convenient medium of exchange. It's not too difficult to understand when we look at the matter clearly, and learning to see clearly is a spiritual exercise.

Major funding for the ministry comes from the supporting members who comprise the CSA *Inner Circle*. About two-thirds of the annual budget is made possible by dedicated people who choose to be so involved. The remainder is realized through book sales and from donations given during seminars and retreats. When I travel to speak for groups, any income realized is deposited into the CSA general fund, to meet ongoing needs. For many years it has been my policy to receive only a modest salary; all lecture honorariums, and proceeds from sales of my books, go directly to CSA.

Once, while being interviewed on television, I was asked, "Why do you do what you do?" I had to pause, because I had never thought about it before. The only answer I could give, which was and is true, was, "Well, it's just what I do. It's what I've always done."

Over the years I have learned to reserve time for rest and recreation, not always as often as I should. I was once asked, "What drives you to keep up the pace, to keep on writing, traveling, and doing the things you do?" An answer came without my having to think about it: "I'm not driven; I'm led. *Someone* is leading me."

Interior, CSA Shrine of All Faiths and Sacred Initiation Temple.

The influence of the ministry extends beyond surface appearances. Hundreds of ministers and leaders representing various New Era teaching traditions receive *Truth Journal* magazine on a regular schedule, and some also support the ministry with occasional financial contributions. Many tell me they derive inspiration from the publications, and that they frequently use material to share with their own groups. For years we have purchased space for advertising in magazines and newspapers which have a readership attuned to New Era ideals. The direct response is seldom sufficient to meet costs, but the purpose is to reach out, to offer a helping hand. I believe in the printed word. It was through an announcement in a magazine that I first learned of *Autobiography of a Yogi*, many years ago. It was the point of contact for me with my guru. It made a difference in my life and, because of that, in the lives of thousands.

Perhaps because of an early fundamentalist Christian involvement, or because of soul destiny, or both, I have always enjoyed seeing a really well-prepared preacher preach. I know that emotion can sometimes get in the way of reasonable doctrine once "revival fires" begin to burn, but every now and then the "spirit of God" takes over and power is evident, with results following.

In 1952, while still minister of the SRF center in Phoenix, I was invited by a member to attend a tent meeting. The Reverend Oral Roberts preached that night to over ten thousand people. Sitting in one of the front rows, I watched him carefully. I could not see anything except one of God's own, letting God pour out to meet needs. In one of Reverend Roberts' books, he told of his early years, and of the advice his mother had given him when he responded to the call to minister. She said, "Oral, you've been called. Let me give you some advice. Always be humble. And promise never to touch the gold or the glory."

This is the most honest advice I know for anyone who feels called to minister. Without humility, God cannot flow through a person. Attraction to results, and attachment to externals, will only cloud one's vision and interfere with des-

Interior of CSA Library and Research Center.

tined purpose. It is also useful advice for anyone, in any situation in life.

New buildings have been constructed on the CSA property from time to time. A well-planned library is certainly important wherever people gather to learn, and when the time was right the CSA Library and Research Center evolved. A member wanted to build a house on the grounds, with the understanding that CSA would have to approve the buyer if she ever chose to sell. A dome-style house was contracted for, but the member later decided not to complete the project. Would CSA accept part of what she had paid on the building as a donation, and assume the remainder? Yes, it could be done. A few weeks later a large truck arrived with the prefabricated parts for the structure. A local contractor was hired, resident trainees were invited to participate and, within a few days, the building was completed.

The Library houses a selection of books to meet almost any need and stacks of magazines representing many areas of interest. A man once visited the center for the first time. His wife had asked him to spend a weekend at Lakemont, and he was not too comfortable with the idea. She was a Yoga student and he was an investment counselor, without any background of study in Yoga or New Thought. When I saw him the morning after their arrival he was relaxed and smiling. His wife said, "Do you know what made the difference? He went down to the library last night, just to look around, and found copies of *Fortune* magazine. When he spotted some *Forbes* magazines he really got comfortable!"

Activities for children have been a regular part of programs here for many years, almost always scheduled in early July, and open to youngsters aged three to twelve. Bill and Doris Isely, a couple devoted to the spiritual life, for several years assumed responsibility for providing facilities and supervision for the children. Doris brought with her many years of experience as a Montessori teacher. The Montessori system, created by Maria Montessori, an Italian educator born in 1870, stresses the ideal of providing a learning environment in which children can be self-educated as a result of sensory involvement with

With the children during Family Week at CSA Lakemont.

special projects. During Children's Week, the adults are offered a program to supplement their retreat experience, while the children are fully involved with sessions in Hatha Yoga, devotional chanting, nature studies, and a variety of creative projects. They are also taught how to experience meditation.

In late 1982, my thoughts turned to the year to come. I began to jot down some ideas, and among them was an idea that "felt good." I drew a quick sketch of an eight-sided structure. One side would have double doors and serve as the entrance. Each of the remaining walls would have a stained-glass window of original design representing, respectively, Christianity, Judaism, Buddhism, Hinduism, Taoism, Islam and Zoroastrianism. The building would be small, twenty-four feet from wall to wall, with walls nine feet high and the ceiling rising at the center. Thus the CSA Shrine of All Faiths and Sacred Initiation Temple was conceived.

Early in the new year I contacted a local contractor and obtained from him an estimate of costs for the building. Soon after the project was announced to our membership the funds were available, and the Shrine was dedicated in July of 1983. The stained-glass windows were designed and made by a local artist, who seemed to intuit exactly what I had in mind. The finished result is beautiful. The Shrine is used by visitors as a quiet meditation place; occasionally it is used for weddings, christenings, and when initiating individuals or small groups into Kriya Yoga procedures.

It was early in 1977 that I experienced a vivid premonition that the ministry would unfold rapidly, with international influence. I inwardly accepted this possibility and left the results to God. That year, three events occurred which proved right my earlier premonition.

Now that we had a comfortable meeting facility in the new Meditation Hall, we announced programs to take place from May to September, with weekend and weeklong sessions being offered to accommodate the needs of students. One of the weeklong programs offered was for training as teachers in the field.

During the first Teacher Training Program, an attractive

With CSA ministers, Frankfurt, West Germany. Left to right: Mr. and Mrs. Jurgen Wolf, myself, Rosemarie Schneider, Lotte Riese, Mr. and Mrs. Heinze Stockl, Mr. and Mrs. Hans-Joachim Bitterhof. (1985)

Dr. Eniang E. Offiong, leader of CSA activities in Nigeria, and Mr. Samuel Sasu, founder of CSA West Africa, Ghana.

woman from Germany attended. She was quiet and attentive and, for the most part, seemed to be monitoring the proceedings. When the week was over I talked with her at length. She introduced herself as Rosemarie Schneider, from Frankfurt, Germany, and informed me that she was here to look me over, to see if what was taught at CSA was "as clear and as true as I've found some of your books to be."

Her story unfolded. A few years before, she had come across a copy of *Die Macht der Seele*, the title given to *This Is Reality* in the German edition. She had carefully studied the book and worked diligently to apply what she learned. Since at that time none of my other books were available in the German language, she obtained them in English and read them by comparing the words to an English-German dictionary. She still maintains that she learned to read English in that way.

Rosemarie asked for permission to translate two of my books into German and to arrange for my lecture visit to her country. I agreed to her proposal. When she returned to Germany, she gathered some friends around her and set to work. CSA Europa was founded and incorporated in Germany as a non-profit foundation organized for the public good, with education as the emphasis.

When all plans were firm, CSA Europa invited me to speak in several cities in Germany. What an enthusiastic reponse in every city visited! Posters announcing the public lectures had been placed in strategic places, advertisements were placed in the newspapers, leaders of various groups gave full support, and the auditoriums were filled wherever we went. I spoke in English and Rosemarie translated. Bilingual people who were there told me that she did a perfect job in conveying exactly the meaning of the message. In each city, I asked for a show of hands to see how many present had read *Autobiography of a Yogi* in the German-language edition. Invariably, well over half of those present had done so.

An annual tour of European cities has been a regular event every year since that first visit. Not only cities in Germany, but Berne and Zurich in Switzerland and Vienna in Austria are visited. All of the CSA literature is now also published in Ger-

many and is available through many bookstores, in study
groups, by mail, and when public meetings are held. *CSA Magazin* is mailed to thousands of readers six times a year. Printed
lessons are sent to supporting members. A permanent office
is established, with a full-time paid staff.

In 1983 CSA Europa hosted the first European International New Thought Alliance Congress in Frankfurt. Over six
hundred people attended. Approximately seventy-five people
from the United States toured many cities in Europe before
concluding their visit at the Congress. Dr. Blaine Mays, President of INTA, led the tour group. The Reverends Sig and Jane
Paulson, of Houston Unity, participated, along with many
leaders of other truth organizations. It was a spiritually useful
moment of coming together. The International New Thought
Alliance also convenes annual programs in major world cities.

To make possible my first visit to Germany, CSA Europa
had borrowed many thousands of dollars from supportive
friends in order to pay for book printing, advertising, hall
rentals and my hotel and travel costs within Europe. CSA
Lakemont assumed the cost of my roundtrip flight from
Atlanta to Frankfurt. After two years, CSA Europa was financially strong enough to also purchase my airline ticket, and
they are now fully self-supporting. Besides all of my books,
they also publish a few titles by Ernest Holmes, and they stock
titles in German by many authors.

Rosemarie started with a dream, and through diligent
effort and emphasis on service to others the ministry has flour-
ished. Several ordained ministers now offer programs in their
respective geographical areas there, and many home study
groups gather weekly.

Also during the summer of 1977, a young couple visited
here during a retreat program. I was informed that they were
on their way to Japan, where the husband was to be stationed
at a naval installation. I provided them with the addresses of
Seicho-No-Ie centers, and asked them to pay my respects to
Dr. Taniguchi if they had a chance to meet him. A few months
later I received word that they had indeed met Dr. Taniguchi,
and that during their visit with him he had turned to an aide

Beryl and Ellen Hooper, founders and co-ministers of Center for Spiritual Awareness, Northern California Chapter, Los Gatos, California.

and said, "We should invite Mr. Davis to come to speak for us again." Shortly after receiving this information from the couple, a letter arrived here from Seicho-No-Ie, inviting me to again tour Japan.

The third instance of international outreach with its origins in 1977 would include several West African countries. In late December, while writing an article in my home office, I heard a knock at the front door. Opening the door, I was greeted by a smiling black man who said, "Sir, my name is Samuel. I'm from Ghana and I've come to study with you!"

Samuel Sasu lived on the property for the next eighteen months and returned to his home city of Accra, Ghana, to found CSA West Africa. He immediately began to organize lectures and classes in Ghana and Nigeria, with fine response. After a few years, a permanent building was constructed by CSA West Africa members, to serve as a meeting hall and educational center. We have sent regular shipments of books and literature to West Africa for years, as our contribution to the ministry there. Because of the overwhelming response to these books, a book dealer, Mr. Peter Oye of Lagos, Nigeria, began to publish some of my books, with my permission, in order to have sufficient quantities to meet the demand.

While Samuel was with us, he participated in all programs and worked in several departments of CSA in order to become familiar with the procedures necessary to maintaining a ministry. His cheerful demeanor endeared him to all of us, and I knew that he would be successful in the work once he returned home. The work he has done in his part of the world will continue to bless many, for generations to come. The inspiring thing about Samuel, as with Rosemarie, is that he knew what could be done and he entered fully into the process. That is the one thing I have attempted to instill in all of the ministers who represent this teaching emphasis. It is my experience, after more than three decades of ministering, that if one will go forth with faith, and hold nothing back, the Power greater than we are will do the rest.

I am sometimes asked if I will ever retire from the ministry. How does one retire from one's relationship with God? Is there anything else I would rather do? I have never thought of doing anything else. Many years from now, I will not travel as much, and by that time there will be capable CSA teachers who will be able to assume much of the public work. We have never attempted to duplicate the work already being done by other organizations, such as Self-Realization Fellowship, Unity, Religious Science, and the many independent movements. Soul needs are met through various ministries, and all God-centered ministries are essential to our times. Paramahansaji used to say, "The world is a big place, and there is room for everyone." When he said that, he was referring to the many teachers who, while perhaps stressing a different emphasis than he, were still meeting needs. I share that view. There is no need for any sense of competition among truth teachers, whatever the emphasis or tradition. It is God meeting all needs, in ways which best serve, when sincere teachers respond to His call to serve.

For years there has been warm friendship and mutual sharing with many in the work. I count, as friends in God, many ministers in the New Thought tradition and many representatives of the Yoga tradition. After I have been speaking for a Unity or Religious Science church, a person may approach me and say, "Why, you sound just like our own teachers, the way you explain things!" A few days later I may be offering a program at an ashram, leading Sanskrit chanting and speaking on Vedanta. Someone will come up to me and say, "I never met an American before who made me feel so comfortable about practicing Yoga."

A ministry is not an organization; a ministry is God flowing to meet needs. So long as we serve useful purposes we will continue, and when useful purposes are no longer served, then new unfoldments will take place. Individuals and institutions come and go, but the move of God in the world continues through one channel of expression or another.

I can honestly say, concerning this ministry, that I feel no personal sense of accomplishment. I have, I hope, been attentive to duty, and I have followed inner guidance as that guidance has made itself known. I have never wanted anything for myself except understanding, and the inner satisfaction of knowing that I am in my right place, doing what God wants me to do. We do not have to struggle to attain; we have but to be open to the flow, and learn to respond to the inner inclination of life to express and fulfill itself.

This ministry activity is dedicated to supporting people who want to experience a personal relationship with God, in order to let His will be done.

There are many needs to be met in the world. If we can learn to cease thinking about what *we* want, and think in terms of filling needs, we will have no problem in experiencing a sense of meaning and purpose in our lives.

TEN

Our Awakening World: The Promise of the Ages

Planetary consciousness is currently undergoing a dramatic process of transformation, leading to an era when enlightenment will be reflected through the consciousness of humanity. What is now emerging is the fulfillment of prophecy, the promise of the seers of the ages.

Sent forth into manifestation as the result of an urge starting within the Oversoul, the universe is self-nourishing and self-regenerating, because of an innate inclination in the direction of completion. When a sufficient percentage of the world's population is conscious enough to live in harmony with natural laws, cooperation with the forces of the universe will be assured and a human society in which righteousness is spontaneous will prevail.

During our present time-cycle, we are witnessing the unveiling of predestined events. The cosmic clock is running on time. Immature prophets with obscured vision see only external happenings, unaware of trends which are evident to those who perceive, with the eye of knowledge, the workings of a higher Power. Man often vainly presumes that he alone is responsible for every unfoldment of world affairs and for the future of Planet Earth. Little does he know that he is neither master nor pawn, but a participant. As a participant, he has a personal responsibility for the performance of his duty; the major participant in the world process, however, is God.

Almost every culture of which we have record has given birth to the dream of a future ultimate good for mankind and the world. A Golden Age has been predicted by seers, poets, and dreamers of idealistic dreams for ages. Many of the world's religious traditions keep alive the hope of a New Era to come, a veritable heaven on earth in which war will be no more and the peoples of that glad condition will enjoy peace, happiness, prosperity and an intimate relationship with the Creator.

Behind the facade of bravado, rhetoric, and noble assertions, behind the fragile veneer of pretended security and inner calm, there exists in the hearts of many people a deep concern for their fate in the near future. Why is this? Is it because we all sense that something, overshadowing the magnitude of anything we have previously known or experienced, is taking place? I think so. We can feel it deep down, at a level which gives support to a conviction of certainty.

Are we living in the "end times"? Are events tumbling over one another with such maddening speed that we can no longer comprehend what is happening? Will there be a devastating nuclear war? Will the international monetary system collapse and impoverish us all? Will famine ride roughshod over the planet? Or will cataclysmic earthquakes do us in? These are but a few of the questions which arise in the mind from time to time, whether articulated or not.

What are we to do, and where shall we turn? Perhaps a cozy spiritual community will meet our needs, offer us safe haven and enable us to ride out the storm? Or perhaps, just perhaps, what they say is true, and the messiah will appear at the last moment and set virtue on her seat again. When and if he does, he'll punish the wicked, those who got us into this mess. These and other thoughts surface, and if you haven't experienced them, chances are you have heard them expressed by others.

Several years ago, during the summer of 1980, news media carried stories which were depressing, to say the least. One

headline often used was, *Obituary Writers Turn to the Earth.*
Contents of the reports stirred controversy in world capitals
and among concerned individuals and groups everywhere. In
brief, this is what millions of people were told by the various
information sources: *"If present trends continue*, the world in
the year 2001 will be more crowded, more polluted, less stable
ecologically, and more vulnerable to disruption than the world
in which we now live. Serious stresses involving population,
resources and environment are clearly visible ahead. Despite
greater material output, the world's population will be poorer
in many ways than they are today." That was the conclusion
stated in a report made to the President of the United States
by thirteen government agencies at the end of a three-year
study.

Current trends, so the report stated, indicate a growth in
world population at a rate of one hundred million annually.
The economic gap would widen between the rich and the poor.
World oil production would reach its limits and new energy
sources would have to be found. Water resources might become
erratic as world population doubled and forests were diminished. Faulty use of available farmlands might continue. Concentration of carbon dioxide and ozone-depleting chemicals
were expected to increase at rates that could warm the world's
climate to the point of melting polar ice caps. Many of the
conclusions shared in the report were drawn by honest people
who had examined data available to them.

It is certainly necessary to take a global view of conditions
and to intelligently plan for near and distant future needs. We
are increasingly becoming aware of the fact that we are not
isolated from the larger world. The planet is really a global
village in which whatever takes place in any one area extends
its influence everywhere. It used to be believed that it would
take a long time, if ever, for causes in one area of the planet
to be felt as effects elsewhere on the planet. Now, because of
scientific research and almost instant communications capabil-
ities, we are finding out that what may seem an insignificant
occurrence in one area of the planet can have far-reaching
effects, perhaps on a global scale. I speak here of seeming ma-

terial causes and effects as most people know them. What is not generally known, although it is becoming more obvious, is that mental states and states of consciousness also influence the human condition and happenings on the planet.

In 1984, a massive report was published in book form under the title *The Resourceful Earth*, edited by Julian L. Simon, a colleague of the late Herman Kahn. Almost two dozen papers were included in the volume, the findings and conclusions assembled by scientists and others long concerned with the future of Planet Earth. The report largely refuted the 1980 government report mentioned above, while admitting that necessary steps must be taken to see to the nourishing of the planet and the welfare of its inhabitants.

It is useful for such information to be shared, even if there is disagreement about conclusions and possible solutions, because one result can be to awaken consciousness and encourage responsible action. On the other hand, when predictions are alarmingly dire, an attitude of despair tends to spread through public consciousness, causing a feeling of helplessness in the average person. He assumes himself incapable of doing anything to improve conditions and continues to concentrate his energies upon coping with life's problems as they present themselves in his immediate environment, while leaving solutions to larger issues to the presumed experts. And, thankfully, the planet is blessed with a great many intelligent and caring men and women who are involved with research and problem-solving.

According to many seers, we are now pulling free from the last Dark Age cycle, and moving in the direction of an Age of Enlightenment, which will flower on Planet Earth a few thousands years from now. Currently we are but in the early dawn of that Age, but with the emergence of each new day there is always hope—hope and the possibility of good things to be experienced.

An *era* is a duration of time marked by distinctive characteristics and events. History records many such durations, and today we have access to a considerable body of data concerning them. With the increase of intelligence now manifesting, along with spiritual awakening, among the peoples of the world, we are fast discovering things about life in the universe which were not previously known except to a special few. I well recall, as a small child, hearing ministers and Sunday school teachers assert that creation began exactly six thousand years ago and that everything that has occurred until now has unfolded during those six thousands years. I never once heard a word of disagreement from anyone in the congregation!

Latest estimates place the age of the universe at between fifteen and twenty billion years, and billions of years yet remain before this known universe is withdrawn into the unmanifest field. We can see in the geologic records left on the planet evidence that millions upon millions of years of continuing change and transformation have occurred, and the process is continuing. How could it not continue—the universe is a living organism! What we are now discovering fills the rational person with a feeling of awe and wonder. The supremacy of spirit over mind, and spirit, through mind, over matter, is more and more being comprehended. We are exploring, simultaneously, inner space and outer space, with surprising and satisfying results. More and more ancient truths are understood as being valid. The quest to understand the unified field, the basic underlying *something* from which all things emerge and by which all things are made possible, is nearer to fulfillment. Along with discovery, along with comprehension of what is really behind this world of shifting appearances, there emerges a sense of respect and of moral responsibility. This is part of the awakening process in our current era.

Yes, we are living through the end of an old cycle and the beginning of a new one, a more inviting one for all who are conscious enough, and appreciative enough, to be a part of the process. Fast-moving events are evidence of rapid change. To answer the questions listed earlier, there will be no global nuclear war; the international monetary system will not collapse; the food needs of all people on the planet will be met; earthquakes will occur, not because of man's sinful nature, but because they have always occurred when shifts of the planet's plates require it. Man will not, *cannot*, remove himself from the planet through disaster or disregard for essentials. A higher Power is in charge, and has ever been in charge, of the affairs of the universe.

Never mind the prophets of doom. What do they know about God, the order of the universe, and the purpose of it all? Listen to the voice that speaks to you from your innermost essence; listen to the call to reason, and the unmistakable assurance of the soul's intuition. Then, armed with faith and hope, firm in the knowledge that you are destined to be a part of the grand drama now unfolding, enter into the process with gladness and thanksgiving for the opportunity to play your allotted role. Let emotions be constrained by judgment, let actions be guided by wisdom. Let love rule.

Above all, be constant in the cultivation of the virtues, and faithful to prayer and quiet contemplation. The seat of righteousness and the Author of all that is truly worthwhile, will then surely find free and unrestricted expression through you. Your days will not cease until you have seen the fulfillment of your most idealistic dreams, and a world whose awakening is without end.

APPENDIX

The Philosophy and Science of Yoga

That knowledge of Consciousness can be experienced is the central theme of all enlightenment traditions. The essence of man is spirit; therefore, all knowledge is resident within every person. Outer attempts to acquire understanding are useful only to the degree that the experience confronted outwardly results in inner recognition and comprehension. When knowledge of the nature of Consciousness is experienced, knowledge of God, souls, the world process, and the purpose of life is experienced. Sometimes, knowledge is experienced in a succession of insights; at other times everything is known during a flash of revelation.

The average person does not know his real nature because he is presently incapable of error-free perception. He thinks himself to be a personality, individualized and separate from the One Life. While this seems to be true for the one who is experiencing this error in perception, it is not true, because man's essence is divine, a particularization of Supreme Consciousness. It is as though various reflections of the sun, in a pool of water, were to consider themselves as having independent reality, unaware of the truth that they are but reflections of that which is the cause of their existence.

Assuming itself to be a self-sufficient individualized being, the soul is under the spell of delusion, and all other problems common to the human condition then follow: pride, attachment, aversion, overinvolvement with sensory experiences, and all of the mental and emotional conflicts too varied to describe.

How does the soul, desirous of understanding and freedom, go about the process of awakening which results in knowledge? The masters of spiritual perfection, for centuries, have taught the same basic procedure: one who is deluded must repent, experience a change in attitude and outlook, and look away from the personality-self to the Source.

Helpful to one on the spiritual path is frequent examination of the philosophical teachings of enlightened souls. It is rare that a person is able to comprehend the final truth about life immediately upon reading or hearing about it. Repeated study and analysis, however, will eventually result in soul recognition and true insight.

One of the major philosophical systems of India is that of *Samkhya*; the word refers to *enumeration, or numbering, of aspects and stages of manifestations of Consciousness*, from the Transcendental Field through all extensions and involvements, resulting, finally, in material creation.

Twenty-five divisions and categories are explained as the basis of involution and evolution. When the total process is clearly comprehended, one then knows that there is but one Life, one Being, one Power, and one Substance.

1.*The Unmanifest Field of Consciousness* —The Absolute, Transcendental Reality which is beyond the most subtle levels of creation. It is the source of all manifestation and the reality of all that is. The source of all that is, and the knowledge of it, can never cease to be, for it is stable, pure, without beginning. It is unmodified pure existence. All of the forces of nature emerge from this field and eventually flow back into it.

This field of Consciousness can be experienced during moments of mind-transcendence, during incidents of unexpected insight, and as the result of intentional meditation.

2. *Initial Manifest Consciousness* —This is the field of Consciousness known as the Godhead, the omnipresent Self of all souls. In the Godhead are polarities, and modifications known as the *gunas*, the electrical attributes. Every manifestation of Consciousness, this side of the Absolute, is endowed with attributes without which no manifestation would be possible.

When the electrical attributes of the Godhead are in a condition of equilibrium, material creation does not exist. The potentialities for material creation remain contained in the Godhead until the electrical attributes are no longer in balance; then the attribute of heaviness, *tamas guna*, causes an expansion in the direction of material creation.

This is the outbreathing of God which makes possible the worlds. During the phase of inbreathing, the universe is drawn back into the field of God. This process is incomprehensible to unenlightened man, but it can be experienced during meditation. Many seers have testified to having inwardly "seen" the manifestation and the dissolution of universes. Since souls come out of the field of God, the knowledge of the process is innate.

The periodic process of involution and evolution occurs because of natural law. Neither process is due to any arbitrary whim of the Godhead.

3. *Initial Movement in the Direction of Manifestation* — When forces within the Godhead expand in the direction of material manifestation, energy forms as substance and life units become involved as souls. The aspect of God which directs the process and regulates it, is referred to by Christians as *the Christ of God*. Various are the names men use to identify God and His aspects, but beyond names is that Reality which we are now examining.

4. *The Further Involvement of Consciousness* —The outflowing force which makes possible every manifest thing is the Word (OM or AUM). It is behind and through all creation, as the Substance by which everything is made possible and of

which it is formed. It manifests as the creative current, fine particles which make possible combinations of life-units, as time, and as space. A single force exists; all other forces in nature are but aspects of it.

Consciousness is omnipresent and omniscient, everywhere present and everywhere aware. Consciousness is omnnipotent, the all-pervading power. Consciousness enlivens every organism, and Consciousness is the stuff of which nature is formed. Unenlightened people often move frantically about, attempting to discover God. God is all there is, and God is right where any person is. The problem before us is not that we do not know where to look for evidence of God's reality; rather, it is that we often do not know "how" to look at the obvious.

Life is a play of Consciousness, a dance of Spirit and nature, both aspects of one Thing. Maleness and femaleness interact to make creation possible. Consciousness as the Godhead is referred to as Father, and Consciousness expressing as creation is referred to as Mother. Without male and female involvement, birth cannot occur.

5. *Cosmic Mind* —Mind is a term used to refer to a manifest aspect of subtle nature through which Consciousness can express. It is to be understood that there is but one Mind, and that a person's mind is but a portion of the one Mind. It is by entering into a creative relationship with Cosmic Mind that we are able to dream dreams true, that we are able to imagine possibilities and see them take form as circumstances and tangible realities. It is through visualization and intention that a conscious person can, to a degree, control natural forces and regulate his life. When this ability is misused, one interferes with the flow of orderly circumstances and causes discomfort to others and himself. For this reason seers teach that one should not be selfishly involved with causing effects through the use of mental abilities.

The "tension" between the positive pole of the Godhead and the negative pole of the outflowing force results in the manifestation of Cosmic Mind. Cosmic Mind pervades the universe and makes possible Cosmic Feeling, Cosmic Particulariza-

tion (as nature), Cosmic Activity and Cosmic Self-Awareness.
The human mind is comprised of four aspects: self-sense (ego),
feeling, thought-forming, and discernment (intelligence).

Paramahansa Yogananda said, "Everything in creation is
taking place in the mind of God. The universe is His dream."
Mystics have often taught that it is useful for one on the spiritual path to learn to dream consciously, and then to relate
the memory of conscious dreams to what is occurring while in
the waking state. In this way one learns to discern a similarity
between sleeping dreams and waking "dreams."

The creative process has purpose; innate to the process is
a self-renewing influence which upholds and maintains nature.
When one is able to be open to this influence, one is then led
along the path of least resistance and experiences unfoldment
after unfoldment. It is then that one experiences grace, good
fortune which is not earned.

6-15. *Ten Connections Between Mind and the World* —
These provide the basis for the five sense perceptions and the
five organs of action. Senses include hearing, feeling (touch),
sight, smell and taste. Organs of action include speech, motion,
excretion, generation, and manual dexterity. These connections have roots in the mind, which is why dreams are often
so vivid. During a dream one can hear, feel, see, smell, taste,
talk, move, do anything that is desired and experience whatever can be experienced during the waking state.

The soul, so this philosophical system teaches, is enveloped in five sheaths. These are: a sheath or "body" of subtle
substance; a sheath of magnetic aura-electricities, the intellectual sheath; the mental covering; a "body" of life-force
(prana); and the physical body. When the average person leaves
the physical body at the time of transition, he takes with him
the four remaining coverings. When an enlightened soul leaves
a body it can, according to its state of consciousness and personal destiny, withdraw from all identification and experience
Pure Being.

16-20. *The Essences of the Objects of Perception* —These are expressed as the five elements which provide the basis for the material world. The essence of sound expresses itself in space, the essence of touch expresses itself in air, the essence of sight expresses in fire, the essence of taste expresses in water, and the essence of smell expresses in earth.

21-25. *The Five Elements Making Up Material Creation* — These are designated as earth, water, fire, air (gaseous substance) and ether (fine matter). Of essences and elements, Shankara, a renowned philosopher-seer who lived in India twelve hundred years ago, wrote in his treatise, *Atma Bodh* (Self-Knowledge):

> The physical body, the medium through which the soul experiences pleasure and pain, is determined by past actions and formed out of the five great subtle elements, which become gross matter when one-half portion of one subtle element becomes united with one-eighth portion of each of the other four.

It is well, I believe, to contemplate the matters before us until we experience direct insight. One of the problems for many sincere truth students is that of not having learned the definitions of basic words and terms. They are, therefore, confused. Because of inner confusion they cannot reason through to a logical conclusion, and they do not know the difference between what is true and what is untrue.

Yoga Science and Self-Realization

Yoga is a Sanskrit word. Its meaning is "to yoke," to join together. Practices include various compatible disciplines which enable one to harmonize conflicting and active currents in the system so that restrictions are eliminated and the reality of the soul can be experienced.

A person who engages in yogic practices can belong to any religious tradition or to none. The various procedures have evolved to meet the needs of people, regardless of psychological disposition or present capacities. All that is required is that one enter fully into the program of practice which best suits his needs. The ideal approach to yogic practice is to be willing to release all that is not useful to one's spiritual unfoldment. One is advised not to think in terms of what will be gained; rather, one is advised to surrender to the processes in order to allow the orderly unfoldment of divine qualities. Among the systems of Yoga are the following: (and they are not listed here in order of importance or value. Any approach to God-realization which is correct for the individual is of value to him.)

Hatha Yoga — *Hatha* means sun-moon and refers to the purpose of the practice, which is to result in a harmonizing of internal forces so that transcendence can be experienced. Although body movements (asanas) and other processes are practiced, Hatha Yoga is not merely a system of physical exercises. The gentle twisting and stretching of the body during the practice of yogasanas contributes to improved muscle tone, improved circulation of blood and lymph fluids, a toning of the nervous system, and psychological changes as a result of rigid body conditions being dissolved. Psychological states often result in physical symptoms, and the dissolving of these symptoms through Hatha Yoga practice can result in internal transformation. Included in the Hatha Yoga system are breathing exercises which enable one to regulate the flow, and the force of flow, of nerve force, as well as the subtle life-force (prana). The end result is kundalini awakening, meditation, and samadhi. While it is perfectly acceptable for one to practice Hatha Yoga procedures for the immediate health benefits, let it be understood that the intended purpose is to assist the seeker on the path in his quest to experience liberation of consciousness.

Bhakti Yoga, the Way of Love and Devotion —To truly respect others, and all that is beheld in nature, without judgment, is to love without motive, to love in a pure way. All

negative conditions will dissolve as a result of divine love. To
"love" God while "hating" the world is foolish. To love some
people while faulting others is ignorance. This manifest world
is a divine creation; it is the body of God. All people are divine,
and should be treated as such. This is the way of love.

Devotion to one's chosen aspect of God softens the heart
(dissolves ego) and opens the mind to receive grace. "Not my
will, but Thine, be done," is the prayer of one who is surrendered to God. Even the masters remain open to God's will.
That is why they are liberated. They want nothing for themselves; they are totally open to what God wants to do through
them, and as them.

Karma Yoga, the Way of Selfless Action —*Karma* is the
word used to define cause and effect. Whatever causes we put
into motion, through thought or deed, must result in certain
effects unless causes are modified or neutralized. We reap
what we sow; we harvest the fruits of our own intentions and
actions, whether consciously or unconsciously implemented.
The ideal, then, is to render service, to work in a useful way,
but not to be overly concerned with end results. The results
will be in divine order if we work with the right attitude. Right
actions contribute to right results. Incorrect actions lead to
non-useful results. This is a basic law of life, and there is no
point in debating the matter. Life is as it is; it is we who must
come to terms with it.

Raja Yoga, the Way of Direct Experience —This is the
"royal way," some say the most direct way, to soul freedom.
The text which serves as an infallible guide to meditators is
Patanjali's *Yoga Sutras*. In this classic handbook can be found
all that is required in order to meditate correctly and to ex-
plore the inner spaces of mind and consciousness.

The "secret" to success in meditation is to renounce the
desire for results and surrender to the process, while remaining
aware and observant. Everything will then occur naturally and
correctly. Whatever is experienced or perceived should be
released, so that what is to follow may be allowed to unfold.

The final experience will be realization of *being*. Along the way there may be perceptions of astral realms, causal realms, even the field of God. Release attachment to anything that is experienced or perceived and final revelation will be assured. This is the testimony of the seers of the ages. It is also my testimony.

Jnana Yoga, the Way of Knowledge —The "way of knowledge" through the use of the faculty of discernment (intelligence) is a precarious way. To be successful on this path one must be aware that intuition is superior to intelligence, but the line between them is so thin that it is often difficult to discern. Shankara, in one of his treatises, wrote, "The soul is the light of Pure Consciousness shining in the faculty of intelligence in man." Contemplate that statement during the tranquil after-meditation phase of your meditation session. Be open to direct experience. Let truth be revealed.

All other Yoga systems are included in the ones listed here, and are a matter of emphasis only. *Laya Yoga* deals with sound and the influences of sound. *Kundalini Yoga* deals with actively working with internal forces. *Tantra Yoga* deals with relationships and coming to terms with the forces of nature. The *Kriya Yoga* path emphasizes the most useful aspects of all yogic procedures.

So long as one is *practicing* Yoga he is involved with a process. Eventually, one will no longer *practice* Yoga, but will embody the virtues, and God will find full expression through the personality and body form. Beyond yogic practice is the condition of being free in the Spirit. This cannot be pretended; it can only be experienced through grace, when all restricting conditions have been removed.

Glossary

Whenever a word's meaning is not understood, comprehension of the theme will be incomplete. Refer to this section often, until words and meanings are clear in mind. Many of the words here used are Sanskrit, which means "polished" or "perfected." It will not be necessary for the average reader to become a Sanskrit scholar, but it will be helpful to understand the meanings of the words.

Absolute. The non-dual field of Consciousness. The Transcendental Field. The "void" of the Buddhist, which is really the absence of modification, but which contains the essence of all possibilities.

Actualize. To "make real" or to bring into manifestation. Capacities are actualized when used and demonstrated. Goals are actualized when they become manifest.

Advaita. Non-duality; the teaching that everything in the manifest realms is an expression of one thing, Consciousness. This is more fully explained in the Appendix.

Ahamkara. The ego, or personal sense of being separate from God. Because of this initial error in perception the soul erroneously feels itself to be independent of that which is its larger reality.

Akasa. Often spelled "akasha"; the first of five material elements making up the field of manifest nature. Translated into English as "ether," or fine substance. The remaining four elements are air, fire, water, and earth (gross particles).

Ananda. Literally, bliss. Often used as part of a monastic name by yogis. Example: Yogananda, "bliss through Yoga, or divine union."

Asana. Pose or posture. Yogasanas are the various poses assumed in practicing Hatha Yoga. Sitting poses are used for meditation. The ideal pose for meditation is upright and steady, so the body is comfortable and not inclined to waver while one is absorbed in quiet contemplation.

Ashram. A quiet secluded place for study and spiritual practice. Ideally, an ashram should provide an environment in which residents can live close to nature and where outside distractions are not possible. Only elevating influences should prevail, so that all of the virtues are naturally encouraged to unfold.

Atma. The divine Self of every person. It is this divine Self which is to be consciously realized by the seeker on the spiritual path. When realization is experienced, one knows the true Self to be cosmic, even while assuming various viewpoints, known as souls.

Avadhut. A supremely enlightened person who functions through mind and body while simultaneously being aware of omnipresence. In his later years, after experiencing transcendental states of consciousness, Paramahansa Yogananda told close disciples, "From now on I will appear to be as before, I will relate to you through this personality, but this personality is not the real me."

Avatar. The descent of divine power into human form. A full incarnation of God. Usually such manifestations are for the purpose of infusing planetary consciousness with divine influence. Sometimes avatars play a dramatic role; at other times they remain unknown to those around them. Their redemptive work is purely in line with God's will. Some work with the public, others remain in seclusion. It is entirely a matter of God's will.

Avidya. The word means "not knowledge," in contrast to the word *vidya*, which means full knowledge of Consciousness.

Ayurveda. Science of life. Said to have its basis in life itself, therefore without beginning. According to mythology, the science of Ayurveda passed from the gods to man. Chinese medicine is also believed to have been passed down from a previous Golden Age, and there is a similarity between Ayurvedic and Chinese medical procedures. Both include a total examination of the patient—pulse, temperature, skin condition, condition of the eyes, psychological makeup, and other factors, when making a diagnosis. Ayurveda uses diet, herbs, water therapy, massage, attitude training, detoxification procedures, and other procedures to encourage restoration of the body to a condition of balance. The *Charaka Samhita*, a famous Indian medical text, was preserved for generations by oral tradition before being written down. Using Sanskrit, practitioners of Ayurveda would memorize key phrases and in this way retain the knowledge of their science, as well as pass it on to qualified successors. First put into writing during the first century A.D., the *Charaka Samhita* lists over five hundred herbs and their medicinal uses. Knowledge of Ayurvedic procedures passed from India to Mediterranean countries and finally to the West. During the many years of British rule, state patronage resulted in a decline of Ayurvedic practice in India and Western medicine became dominant. Now, however, there are once again several schools of Ayurveda in India, and scientific research is being used to prove the usefulness of many of the procedures.

Bhagavad Gita. "God's glorious celestial song." A much-loved scripture in which Krishna, a divine incarnation, explains to Arjuna, his disciple, the philosophy of "the eternal way of righteousness" and the way to freedom in God. The reverent reading of the *Gita* cannot fail to result in a profound impact upon the mind and consciousness of the reader.

Bhagavan. Lord. Literally, one endowed with the six attributes: infinite spiritual power, righteousness, glory, splendor, knowledge, and renunciation.

Bhakti. Intense devotional love for God which results in understanding and respect for all of creation. A common teaching of yogis is that love for God leads to knowledge, and knowledge of God results in love.

Brahma. The initial expanding and projecting aspect of the Godhead which results in creation.

Brahmacharya. Spiritual discipline which enables one to acquire control over vital forces and mental and emotional tendencies.

Brahmaloka. The abode of God, corresponding to the highest sphere or realm this side of the Transcendental Field. According to Vedic teachings, only the Transcendental Field is pure, without characteristics of any kind, and everything this side of It is endowed with characteristics and influences, including the field of God.

Brahman. The Supreme Reality, the Absolute.

Brahma Sutras. Also known as the *Vedanta Sutras.* Revelations and philosophical speculations of the seers of Vedic times. Sutras, "threads," are concise statements designed to share understanding and to be contemplated by the student so that the student comes to experience his own revelation about the theme mentioned. Massive commentaries have been written on various sutras which have been compiled.

Buddha. A man who lived in northern India about 500 B.C. Of royal birth, as a young man he became troubled when he saw the sufferings of the average person in society. Leaving home after marrying and fathering a son, he practiced extreme yogic procedures. Later he adopted the "middle way," the way of controlled moderation. He attained illumination and, thus, his name, "The Enlightened One," the Buddha. After his illumination he walked up and down the Ganges Valley for almost fifty years, preaching freely to all and forming a society of renunciate monks. He taught love, non-hatred, dedication to truth, the elimination of wishful thinking, and non-dependence on anything external, including religious ceremony. Illumination, as Buddhists teach, is not a state of consciousness, but the realization of the True Self which is common to us all.

Buddhi. The faculty of discernment possessed by man; the intellectual capacity. When, through discernment, one comprehends the totality of Consciousness, he is a buddha, an enlightened being. All beings possess a buddha nature because all beings are specialized expressions of Supreme Consciousness. When one knows his nature, instead of *about* his nature, he is spiritually free.

Capacity. The power or ability to receive or contain. The power or ability to do, to exercise abilities.

Chakra. A distribution center in the body through which prana flows. The main chakras, or "wheels," are located as follows: crown chakra, upper brain; spiritual eye, between the eyebrows, and the positive pole of the *medulla oblongata*; cervical chakra, in the spinal pathway opposite the throat; dorsal chakra, between the shoulder blades; lumbar chakra, middle of the back; sacral chakra, small of the back; and coccygeal chakra, the lower extremity of the spinal column. Prana flows into the body through the *medulla*, to the brain, and then down the spinal pathway to nourish the body and direct internal processes. The spiritual eye center is used as a point of focus during yogic meditation.

Downflowing prana changes in frequency as it flows through the chakras in order to perform various functions. The ether element is predominant at the throat chakra. It is here that yogis concentrate when they desire to nourish the body without taking food. In descending order, the air element is predominant at the dorsal chakra, fire at the lumbar chakra, water at the sacral chakra, and earth at the coccygeal chakra. It is possible to stimulate the activity of prana at the different chakras by reciting certain mantras.

Chiti. Supreme Consciousness in its aspect as dynamic creative power.

Chitta. The storehouse of memory, making possible the process of thinking.

Christ. The Christ of God is that aspect of the Godhead which is actively involved with the world process. The Christ of God is often referred to as the "only begotten of the Father" or the first emanation from the Godhead. It is the Lord, or ruler of all that takes place in nature. The Jesus of history was an avatar who fully allowed the Christ of God to express in His life. He said, "I of myself can do nothing; the Father within, he doeth the works."

Consciousness. Consciousness is of two kinds. One, there is the consciousness (awareness) of something. Two, there is the entity of consciousness itself, knowing itself as such, without any object or mirror for itself to be perceived in. The second kind is often referred to as pure consciousness. It is also the ground out of which all forms emerge.

Darshan. The blessing one receives as a result of looking upon a saint. To see a saint is to see divine qualities expressed through another, and to experience divine consciousness.

Deva. A "shining one" or god. Gods and goddesses (devis) are souls which dwell in subtle celestial realms.

Dharma. The upholding influence in nature which supports creation and maintains the evolutionary process. The term also refers to evolutionary order, the way of righteousness. The ideal way to live is to live in harmony with the way of righteousness. In this way we cooperate with the world process and we are upheld by it.

Diksha. Yogic initiation, during which instruction is given in meditation procedure and the guru transmits his spiritual force to the disciple. Instruction may vary, depending upon the teaching tradition represented by the guru, and by what the disciple needs to help him be successful on the path. Sometimes a mantra is given, sometimes pranayama is taught, and sometimes the disciple is instructed to look within and contemplate the true nature.

God. The Supreme Being. The stable aspect of God is Pure Consciousness. When we think of God we usually conceptualize the Godhead, with attributes and capacities. Men have given the Godhead many names; so long as one turns to God, regardless of the name used, one is lifted Godward.

Guna. The three gunas are the characteristics and qualities of all nature. Sattwa guna is the force of equilibrium in nature which translates itself into the qualities of good, purity, harmony, balance, happiness, sympathy, light, virtue and knowledge. Rajas guna is the force of energy and motion in nature which translates itself into the qualities of passion, action, struggle, effort, and desire. Tamas guna is the force of inertia and inconscience in nature which translates itself into the qualities of inaction, ignorance, incapacity, darkness and obscurity. Sattwa guna brings illumination to the mind and impels one in the direction of right action and harmony. Rajas guna encourages one to strive, to resist, to attempt to dominate one's environment, to assert will, to fight, to create, to conquer, and to aspire. Tamas guna binds a person through negligence, error and inaction.

The *Gita* teaches that one should cultivate Sattwa guna to avoid being enslaved by Rajas guna or Tamas guna; one should then rise above the influence of even Sattwa guna by experiencing transcendental awareness.

Guru. Literally, the light that dispels darkness. The guru is considered to be God expressing in human form in order to assist disciples who seek liberation of consciousness. For a disciple to be successful in his efforts on the spiritual path he must please his guru; that is, he must abide by the guru's teachings. If the disciple resists the guru's teachings, if he is immature and self-willed, he is not open to higher instruction, nor to the possibility of transcending ego-consciousness. The guru's function is to show the disciple the way to freedom in God. For this to be possible, the disciple must be willing to rid himself of all that is contrary to Self-realization. Guruseva, service to the guru, is to be considered as service to God. By becoming attuned to the guru's consciousness the disciple experiences attunement to God. By understanding the true nature of the guru, the disciple understands the true nature of God.

Hinduism. The name given by foreign invaders to the religious practices of the people of India. The Sindhu river, flowing into the Arabian Sea, forms part of the western boundary of India. It was known by the ancient Persians as the "Hindu" river. The Greeks borrowed the name, changing it into "Indos," later converted into English as "Indus." The Greeks called the country east of "Indos" by the name of India. Its inhabitants became known as Hindus, and their religion as "Hinduism." Even today, many people in India refer to themselves as Hindus. Those who are more precise refer to their religious philosophy and practice as Sanatana Dharma, "the eternal way of righteousness."

Holy Spirit. The life of God expressed throughout the universe. It is the Holy Spirit aspect of God which enlivens the world, and man.

Imagination. The ability to visualize, or picture in the mind's eye, new and novel possibilities. Imagination differs from daydreaming or wishful thinking only in degree; controlled imagination allows one to clearly define the mental picture.

Islam. Mohammed is the inspired prophet of Islam, which acknowledges the One God and respects all religious endeavors which have a Bible, a book of revealed truth. A true Islamite is dedicated to God and chooses to surrender his life to God.

Isvara. The personal aspect of God which governs and regulates creation. This aspect of God is referred to as the Lord, the ruling influence in nature.

Japa. The repetition of any of the names of God, for the purpose of concentration and meditation. A japmala is a string of beads used to assist in concentration and to count the repetitions.

Jaya. Victory. Often spelled "ji." "Ji Guru!" means "Victory to the guru!"

Jivanmukta. A liberated soul which is still embodied. Traces of karma may yet remain, but the soul is inwardly free and will not have to be reincarnated except it be God's will. Future actions of a jivanmukta are determined, not by karmic compulsion, but by God's will.

Jnana. Knowledge of God.

Judaism. The religious system of the Jewish people.

Kalpa. A cycle of time. Planet Earth experiences periodic changes, resulting in varied conditions for man. One Grand

Cycle is about 24,000 years in duration, with sub-cycles of 4,800 years, 3,600 years, 2,400 years, and 1,200 years. The longest of the sub-cycles is an era of enlightenment, when civilizations flourish and order and harmony are experienced by the people. When order begins to break down, the 3,600-year cycle is experienced, during which time the people's capacity to discern the subtle side of life diminishes. This is followed by the 2,400-year descending phase, and finally the 1,200-year phase. After 1,200 years of Dark Age conditions, then another 1,200-year ascending Dark Age phase unfolds, followed by the other eras in reverse order. The last Dark Age, contrary to some popular teachings, ended about A.D. 1700, and the world is now pulling free of that Age's influences. This is why we are now witnessing rapid spiritual awakening, while humanity longs for the ideal world condition which it knows will unfold. The sub-cycles are referred to as yugas, or ages.

Karma. The law of causation; an action resulting in a reaction. The thoughts we think, the actions we perform, determine our day-to-day experiences. Also, the accumulated mental and emotional conflicts contribute to mental states and states of consciousness. The more God-conscious we are, the less prior causes influence present behavior and circumstances. Traumatic experience can, in some instances, result in impressions being made in the brain and cells of the body, interfering with function. In this way some karmic effects can be transmitted to children; that is, children can inherit the characteristics of the parents. The ideal, for one on the spiritual path, is to be free from karmic influences, and to live spontaneously from the awareness of being. Then whatever is done is done in the most appropriate manner to meet existing needs, and such actions do not bind one to future effects. They are actionless-actions.

Kaya-kalpa. A process undergone by some yogis to reverse the ravages of time on their bodies. A rejuvenation process which involves internal cleansing, the use of certain herbs, prolonged rest, and much meditation. To ensure seclusion, the yogi usually remains in a cave or a dwelling far removed from society. One yogi who underwent the kaya-kalpa process three times finally made his transition when he was over one hundred and eighty years of age. The first time he experienced the process, emerging after several months in seclusion, he appeared to be at least twenty years younger than when he began; his hair had returned to its natural color and he had grown a third set of teeth. It is rumored that there are yogis in the Himalayas who use this process to retain the body for hundreds of years. Chinese folklore also contains stories of the mortal-immortals who have learned to remain forever youthful.

Kundalini. Dormant static force resting in nature and in the body of man. When it awakens in nature, life forms begin on the planet. When it awakens in man, soul qualities begin to unfold. In the average person this force is mostly dormant and the person assumes himself to be a physical body. When kundalini awakens and begins to ascend the path of the chakras, then intellectual capacities are unveiled, intuition awakens, and creativity unfolds.

Love. The attracting influence of God is the supreme expression of love, for it draws souls back to a conscious relationship with the Source. Human beings speak of love of country, love of mankind, love for another, and love as affection, or caring but unemotional friendship. All expressions of love are aspects of the soul's love of God. Love is purifying because it calls forth our best qualities, and demands of us surrender to the highest and best in any relationship.

Mahasamadhi. Conscious transition from the body. *Maha* means "great"; mahasamadhi, then, means the "great" or final samadhi. The term is also used to refer to a shrine which may be erected over the tomb of an enlightened yogi.

Mantra. A meditation mantra serves as an attractive focus of attention, so that attention can be led beyond mental processes to the experience of transcendence. Mantras may also be used to influence forces in nature, and to control and regulate such forces.

Maya. The fabric or "stuff" of which nature is formed. The components of maya are light particles, space, time, and the creative force from which they unfold. One characteristic of maya is that it is form-producing, as a mother is form-producing. Another characteristic is that it is truth-veiling; when a soul is identified too strongly with nature it experiences a diminishing of its intuitive and intellectual capacities, and becomes deluded. Maya is illusory, but it is not "illusion." Man, blinded by overidentification with matter, experiences errors in perception and knows but a portion of the allness of Consciousness.

Meditation. The easy process of relaxing the body and allowing the mental field to become clear. It has nothing in common with mental manipulation or hypnotic practices. Meditation is not a passive experience; it is a conscious, creative process. Patanjali's *Yoga Sutras* remains the most reliable guidebook to meditation practice. His explanation is sometimes referred to as "eight-limbed," because eight stages are explained. These are: Yama, the restraints; Niyama, the observances; Asana, correct meditation posture; Pranayama, regulation of vital forces in the body; Pratyahara, inward turning; Dharana, concentration; Dhyana, contemplation; Samadhi, clear awareness, the peak experience.

Moksha. Liberation of consciousness, resulting in knowledge and freedom from delusion.

Mudra. A symbolic pose or gesture. Also, a yogic procedure used to stimulate vital forces in the body and to afford the yogi conscious control over involuntary processes.

Nada. Different sounds heard within during meditation. These are variations of OM, the primal sound.

Nadi. A channel through which prana flows in the subtle body. For instance, ida is the left channel along the spinal pathway through which the "moon" current flows. Pingala is the right channel through which the "sun" current flows. During the course of a given day the force of flow through these channels will change, resulting in mood shifts and adjustments in states of consciousness. When these currents are in a condition of equilibrium, then prana flows with greater force in the sushumna, the central channel in the spinal pathway, and the mind is calm, allowing for introspection and successful meditation.

Nadi-Shuddi. The purification of the nadis, and the nervous system, as a result of active-flowing prana being encouraged through the practice of certain pranayamas and mudras. This also occurs naturally when kundalini is awakened.

Nirguna-Brahma. Supreme Consciousness without attributes or qualities. Saguna-Brahma refers to Consciousness with attributes and qualities.

OM. The primal sound current from which all other manifestations in nature are evolved. OM is also considered the highest, or most pure, mantra to be contemplated during meditation.

Omnipotence. Unrestricted power, the power of God.

Omnipresence. Present everywhere simultaneously.

Omniscience. Being conscious everywhere.

Paramahansa. The highest spiritual reference given to a Self-realized yogi. A paramahansa is one who can live in the world and be untouched by any of the qualities of the world.

Paramukta. Enlightenment with no trace of karmic involvement. Jivanmukta is enlightenment with seeds of karma remaining. Paramukta is final liberation of consciousness.

Prakriti. Nature, consisting of elements and qualities. Purusha is the divine force which enlivens Prakriti.

Prana. Life force which permeates the universe. Pranas are frequencies of the creative current flowing from the Godhead. When pranas are in harmony in the system, health is natural; when pranas are out of harmony, disease is possible. Pranayamas are procedures used to regulate the force and circulation of prana in the body, usually through regulation of the breathing rhythm.

Prarabdha Karma. Residual karmic patterns which are subject to restimulation and which can cause effects. These can be allowed to express and be exhausted, or they can be neutralized through prayer, meditation, certain yogic procedures, and the superior force of Self-Realization.

Rasa-Lila. The "eternal dance" taking place between the Lord of the universe and souls involved with creation.

Reincarnation. The process of being born into another flesh body after departing one and resting in the astral sphere for a duration. This doctrine is taught by enlightened teachers, so there is no necessity of debating the concept. One is drawn back to the material world so long as there remains attachment to it, or if one has a duty to be performed. Some souls make their transition from the body and continue to work out their spiritual freedom in subtle astral or causal realms, before awakening in God, or experiencing complete transcendence.

Rishi. A seer, one who reveals Truth.

Sadhana. One's spiritual practices and involvement with processes designed to remove inner restrictions and result in

the experience of Self-realization. One can be involved
with such practices wherever he might be, whatever his
station in life. Transformation is an inner process.

Samadhi. When mental modifications no longer interfere with
soul awareness, samadhi is experienced. Samadhi is not an
unconscious trance state, but a state of clear awareness.
Initial samadhi states may be colored by feelings and perceptions. Higher samadhi states are unconditioned. Sahaja
samadhi is perfect soul awareness, even while using mind
and body in a natural way. Samadhi is a state of consciousness; it is not knowledge, although one can acquire knowledge through samadhi if the intention is present.

Samkalpa. Determination, intention with mental conception,
to cause something to come into existence through the
exercise of pure will.

Samkhya. To enumerate, or number. Samkhya is the philosophical system which examines and explains the order of
the universe by precisely describing all aspects of it. Samkhya philosophy is basic to the *Bhagavad Gita* and the
Yoga Sutras.

Samsara. The "forever becomingness" of the world process.
Unenlightened man is caught in the shifting currents of
nature and experiences change whether he wants to or not.
The ideal is to flow with change while being anchored in
eternity.

Samyama. Perfect contemplation, as taught in the third section of the *Yoga Sutras.* Concentration, meditation, and
identification with the object of concentration is perfect
contemplation. In this way, if the intention is to know the
reality of God, this can be known through experience.
Through samyama the yogi acquires siddihis, soul abilities.

Sanatana Dharma. The eternal way of righteousness. Traced to
pre-vedic times, it is said to be without origin, having its

roots in Pure Consciousness, which is without beginning or end. The basic theme is that one should live in harmony with nature, attend to one's duty, and aspire to knowledge of God and Self-realization.

Sanyasin. A renunciate who has taken holy vows for the purpose of devoting all energies to Self-realization and, sometimes, world service.

Shakti. Cosmic creative energy which enlivens the worlds. Also the creative force in man which, when aroused, vitalizes the body and awakens kundalini.

Shaktipat. The infusion of shakti from guru to disciple. This can take place during initiation or anytime the disciple is receptive. Shakti can also begin to stir spontaneously when one is surrendered to God.

Shiva. The aspect of the Godhead which sends forth the worlds and then dissolves them, only to produce them again. Shiva is the patron deity of yogis. Shakti is Shiva's consort; between them the world process is made possible.

Siddha. A "perfected" being, a master of Yoga.

Siddhis. Powers of perfection, the capacities and abilities which unfold when inner restrictions are removed. The third section of the *Yoga Sutras* expounds in considerable detail on the subject of siddhis. Some of the abilities are: the power to be as small as an atom, to be as large as the universe, to be weightless, to see at a distance with remote vision, to do anything that is intended, and to be invincible.

Spiritual Eye. The third eye, the eye of intuition. The focus for this is in the space between the eyebrows. Here a yogi can enter the subtle realms or have mastery over space and time.

Spiritual Mind Treatment. A New Thought term referring to the procedure in which one becomes established in the awareness of God and then inwardly realizes that whatever he wants to see unfold is already accomplished in his mind and consciousness.

Swami. A member of the ancient monastic order reorganized by Shankara in the Eighth Century. A swami is one who has renounced all ties and attachments and roams the world with God as his sole support.

Taoism. The old religion of China, said to have been inspired by the sage Lao Tsu, author of the *Tao Te Ching.* Emphasis is upon tranquillity, non-artificiality, simple enlightenment and non-acting (but letting).

Tattwa. The true or inner essence of a thing. The essence of the senses is the root of the senses in the mind. The essence of anything can be known through samyama, or perfect contemplation.

Transcendental Field. The unmanifest field of pure consciousness out of which all things emerge and into which they dissolve. One who experiences the Transcendental Field during meditation is resting at the very seat of power and creativity. Working from this level, all things in harmony with natural law are possible with minimum effort.

Turiya. The "fourth" state of consciousness transcending the three commonly experienced states of deep sleep, dream state, and ordinary waking state. Superconsciousness.

Upanishads. A collection of sacred texts which have origins in the oral teaching tradition. In centuries past in India, one would live with a guru in a retreat environment and "sit near" him to learn, hence the term, upanishad (upa-near; ni-down; sad-to sit). There are many upanishads, and Shankara wrote commentaries on several of them. These are called the Greater Upanishads because of their higher visibility. The Lesser Upanishads, which Shankara did not write commentaries on, contain advanced yogic instruction meant for the special few who were qualified to understand them. Among the Lesser Upanishads is the *Shandilya Upanishad*, which was composed by one of Lahiri Mahasaya's ancestors. Kriya Yoga procedures are explained in it.

Vasana. Latent tendencies with roots in the unconscious. These tendencies, inclined in the direction of actualization, cause movement in the psyche, often resulting in experiences which are not anticipated. All latent tendencies with the potential to unduly influence should be neutralized, so Yoga teaches.

Veda. Veda refers to that which is self-revealed. The oldest known religious scripture in the world is the *Rig-Veda*. The Vedas contain the revelations of the ancient seers; the Upanishads offer philosophical explanation of them.

Vedanta. The summing up of the wisdom of the vedic tradition. The final wisdom is, "Supreme Consciousness is the cause, reality, and support of all that is."

Viveka. Discrimination between the changeless and the transitory. With discrimination, discernment, one sees without errors in perception.

Vyasa. A sage who is believed to have arranged many of the vedic works in their present form. Vyasa is probably the name used by many sages who worked on the project over the years.

Yama. The restraints recommended for one on the yogic path: harmlessness, truthfulness, non-stealing, regulation of all internal forces, and the absence of greed. The niyamas are the observances: internal and external cleanliness, serenity, intentional self-discipline, study of the nature of consciousness, and surrender of the ego-sense in order to realize the larger true nature, God. These guidelines apply to anyone on the spiritual path, regardless of time or place.

Yoga. To "yoke" or bring together all of the aspects of body, mind and personality, to harmonize conflicting currents in the system so that Self-realization can be experienced.

Zen. The word is a transliteration of Ch'an, the Chinese for the Sanskrit word Dhyana, or contemplation. Dhyana became Ch'an in Chinese and Zen in Japanese. When Buddha attained enlightenment, the highest aspect of that experience could not be compared to anything known or unknown. During the lifetime of Buddha, religion in India had become ritualized. He pointed a way to spiritual freedom that transcended ritual. Some consider him to have been a "spiritual revolutionary" in this regard. It was shortly after this period of history that Shankara emerged to restate vedic principles in the light of knowledge. Buddhist influence moved through Tibet, to China and to Japan, as various sages traveled to spread the dharma, the way of righteousness.

Zoroastrianism. An ethical religious emphasis with roots in Persia (Iran).

INDEX

For additional information about Center for Spiritual Awareness, and a complete listing of literature, books, and services offered, contact: Center for Spiritual Awareness, Box 7, Lake Rabun Road, Lakemont, Georgia 30552.

In West Germany contact: CSA Europa, Kaiser-Friedrich-Promenade 87, D-6380 Bad Homburg, West Germany.

In West Africa contact: CSA West Africa, Post Office Box 507, Accra, Ghana.

For books in Nigeria, contact: Peter Oye Agencies, Post Office Box 5803, Lagos, Nigeria.